Against the Wind

by Marty Basch

Top of the World Communications, Intervale, New Hampshire

AGAINST THE WIND
A Maine to Alaska Bicycling Adventure
By Marty Basch

Published by:
Top of the World Communications
PO Box 731, Intervale, NH 03845

Copyright ©1995 by Marty Basch
First Printing April, 1995
Printed in the United States of America

Library of Congress Catalog Card Number: 95-90226
ISBN 0-9646510-0-9 $12.95 Softcover

For those who have answered the call of the road

Acknowledgments

Although I cycled alone, there were a number of people who were with me during this trip. First and foremost, I would like to thank Jan Duprey for her love, support and carefully packaged treats during the ride. She proves that love comes in pint-sized packages. I also want to thank her for the work she did on this book. She knew how and where to deliver a swift kick when I needed one. A thank you also goes to Jena Duprey. She always had a postcard waiting for me along the way and was constantly concerned about the soreness of my behind.

The newspapers which carried my columns during the adventure also deserve kudos. They allowed me to carry out my desire to travel and write. Thanks to Mark Guerringue, Adam Hirshan and the staff at *The Conway Daily Sun*, Kelly Bostian at *The Fairbanks News-Miner* and Sandy Bucknam and Alan Greenwood at *The Nashua Telegraph*. In cyberspace, I want to thank Tim Oey for the encouragement to post my pieces on America Online's Bikenet.

Peg DegliAngeli designed the book's cover and helped with its production. Her help was invaluable. Thank you to Bruce Luetters for his advice in the production as well. Everett Rowley, who has heard about my desire to write a book for years and endured my babbling about it, finally convinced me to shut up and do it. Thank you.

Mark Fox snapped the cover shot in Summit County, Colorado. Although it wasn't taken during my Maine to Alaska ride, it best symbolizes what long-distance bicycle touring is all about. Debra Michals lent her expertise in editing the book.

I also want to thank Constable Dan Small of the Royal Canadian Mounted Police, Doug Fejes, John Hedden, Chuck and Collette Graham, Judith Kenyon at *The Fort Nelson News*, Ken Stahlnecker and Jobe Chakuchin of the United States Department of the Interior and Eric Fry of *The Seward Pilot Log* for furnishing me with the ends of several tales that began on the road.

Jack Townshend of Fairbanks gets a special thank you. He was following my trip in the newspaper and we met through a serendipitous encounter while I was in Fairbanks. Thanks for all you have done.

Of course, one has to thank his parents. Mitch and Lynn Basch have been behind me 100 percent during my bicycling adventures. I even called them once a week — usually. My grandmother and sister have also been there for me while I've been on the road. Thanks for your support.

There were countless, nameless people who encouraged me during the ride. There was a woman in a car who held out three oranges for me in the Yukon. I thank you. There were several people who topped off my water bottles. Thank you. The people who took me in and fed me, thanks. For those who followed my travels along the information highway, thanks for coming along. Don't worry, Rodeman will ride again.

You never know where you are going to hear a good story. Author Marty Basch (l) sits on the shoulder of the Alaska Highway in the Yukon listening to John Hedden (r) of Sitka, Alaska tell him about the strange experience of meeting a couple who gave him the cremated remains of a relative. Hedden was riding with Joanne Harrison of Aspen, Colorado who took this photo.

Table of Contents

The Beginning

The Cremation of Jinkzie Green

*There are strange things done in the midnight sun
By the men who moil for gold:
The Arctic trails have their secret tales
That would make your blood run cold:
The Northern Lights have seen queer sights,
But the queerest they ever did see
Was that night on the marge of Lake Lebarge
I cremated Sam McGee.*

— From "The Cremation of Sam McGee" by Robert Service

I don't know where my fascination with the Alaska Highway began. The north has always drawn me to it. The north had always been New England for me. Now, New England was a place where people who lived in British Columbia and the Northwest Territories might want to go for a slightly warmer climate.

I wasn't the only person in the summer of 1994 living his dream of traveling to Alaska. There were others, and I met many of them. Some were even on a bicycle, like me.

Jinkzie Green was one of them. Actually, she wasn't *on* the bicycle. She was more of a passenger. Jinkzie wasn't doing much pedaling either. Jinkzie was dead.

Too bad Robert Service was dead, too. Had the Canadian poet been alive that summer instead of during the turn of the century searching for gold in the Klondike, he might have come across Jinkzie.

Not that Jinkzie would have said much to Service. But Jinkzie was doing something Service probably had never done — taken a posthumous bicycle tour of the Yukon and Alaska.

Jinkzie hadn't planned to see the wilds of the north this way. It's safe to say she would have preferred to do it while she was alive. Chances are she wouldn't have done it by bike either. The dear departed Jinkzie was a passenger, tucked neatly into the bowels of John Hedden's panniers.

When I first met Hedden, a junior high school teacher from Sitka, Alaska, I hadn't noticed Jinkzie. There wasn't a toe, finger or elbow protruding from his gear. Nor did his friend Joanne Harrison, a motel manager from Aspen, Colorado, initially say much about her. But it didn't take long for them to tell the tale of "The Cremation of Jinkzie Green."

Hedden and Harrison had left the southeastern Alaska town of Skagway in late June and were on a two month bicycle tour of Alaska and the Yukon. It was late July and the couple was cycling the world famous Alaska Highway. At around milepost 1114 in the Yukon, they decided to call it quits for the day and paid for a campsite at the Pine Valley Motel and Cafe. In those parts, motels also double as a place to pitch a tent.

As Harrison remembered that night, the two had pulled into the campground and began setting up their tent when a woman came over and spoke the words all grubby, exhausted, windburned travelers want to hear: "Would you like to join us for dinner?"

They did.

Cyclists often rely on the kindness of strangers. Road riders are the recipients of many gifts like water, beer, stove fuel, a shower and a free place to stay. One of the most coveted gifts though is dinner. Put together a shower, free place to stay and dinner and that's heaven.

It seems the woman — Marla Green — and her husband — Ron Green — hailed from Chule Vista, California. They were emptying out the refrigerator in their recreational vehicle and had more food than mouths.

Hedden and Harrison marched right on over and the next thing you know they're having lots of food, drinking beer and swapping travel stories. The two bicycling adventurers ate every morsel they could while sitting in the comforts of modern mobility.

As the meal was ending, one of the Greens said to the couple, "How would you like to pay for your dinner?"

Harrison and Hedden looked at each other kind of strangely. They thought the meal was a gift, and now waited uncomfortably as they heard their host's request.

That's when the two were introduced to Jinkzie.

Jinkzie, whose real name was Jennie, was Ron's mother. She had always dreamed of going to Alaska and was a great fan of the author James Michener, especially his book *Alaska*. Jinkzie died before she ever saw her promised land and was then cremated.

But that didn't stop Ron and Marla from getting her there. No way. The Greens were carrying Jinkzie with them in their RV, going about Alaska and scattering pieces of Jinkzie everywhere. A nose here, a toe there; it all looks the same when it's ashes.

Now the Greens were heading home. One place they never made it to though was Sitka. Sitka was a place Jinkzie had wanted to visit. So the Greens asked Hedden if he would take a bit of Jinkzie back home with him. He agreed.

"Now she's seeing Alaska in the after-life," said Harrison during a roadside interview.

Out from the urn Jinkzie came and into an envelope she was poured. The envelope was sealed. To keep Jinkzie safe from the elements, the envelope was deposited into a plastic storage bag. Just to make sure Hedden didn't forget who Jinkzie was, the Greens wrote her name on the outside of the envelope. That way Hedden couldn't mistake Jinkzie for instant onion soup.

This tale was relayed to me on the side of the road in the Yukon, somewhere near Sheep Mountain on a late July afternoon as the two cyclists were keeping an eye on the rain in the sky. Hedden and Harrison weren't the only ones on a bicycle that summer.

So was I.

The duo was heading west on the Alaska Highway, while I was traveling east. As is the custom with bicycling campers, you stop to chat and do the equipment dance. This is when the parties involved pull over to the side of the road and check each other out. In nearly an instant, the eyes and brain process all sorts of information: bicycle brand and make, tire types, clothing, helmet type, size of thighs and calves, types of shoes, handlebar system, growth of beard, brand of eye wear, water carrying

John Hedden (l) and Joanne Harrison (r) carried the cremated remains of Jinkzie Green through the Yukon and into Alaska. The author met the pair while cycling the Alaska Highway. Jinkzie's in the envelope. (Photo by Marty Basch).

system, number of gears, size of chain ring, types of panniers, color of sleeping bag, etceteras.

Then the question and answer session begins. Where are you coming from? Where are you going? Where do you live? How many miles do you do in a day? Did you see so-and-so who was going your way? How many flats did you have? Where is the closest water source, food store, bakery, campsite? Have you had any mechanical problems? Have you seen any wildlife? Where is the nearest laundry? Where are the damn ATM's in this Canadian wilderness? Are there any electrical outlets around so I can charge my computer?

The last question took Hedden and Harrison by surprise. Cyclists tend to notice lots of things along the road as they trudge by at 10 miles per hour.Most of them aren't looking for outlets since they tend to leave their hardware home.

Inside my right rear saddlebag was a laptop computer. It was safe and dry inside a soft case. To protect it from rain, hail and snow, it was then placed into a dry bag, a waterproof sack used by canoeists and kayakers. This was my traveling office.

I explained to the two that I was bicycling the information highway from Maine to Alaska and zapping back weekly columns to three newspapers plus posting the stories on an online service. Hedden and Harrison then began to share some of their experiences. That's how the tale of Jinkzie Green made its way into print.

So there on the damp gravel by the road as cars, trucks and RV's continued their parade to and from Alaska, Hedden and Harrison spun their story as this roving reporter, literally, typed away during the interview.

"She's guiding me," said Hedden when asked what it was like driving Miss Jinkzie. "When I get home, I'm going to hike to the top of Harbor Mountain which overlooks Sitka and scatter her ashes there."

No doubt Jinkzie enjoyed the view.

Into the Wind

Portland, Maine is four time zones and one country away from the Yukon. At Congress Street, the Cumberland and Oxford Canal feeds the waters of the Atlantic Ocean. A graffiti-marred green sign welcomes visitors to the city. On the morning of May 2, 1994, a 32- year-old, mechanically-challenged, 196-pound white male dipped his bicycle wheels into the cold, gray Atlantic while his girlfriend Jan Duprey snapped pictures.

She said something about good luck, you need to do this, don't worry I won't dump you now. She would spend a couple of days traveling along in her Isuzu Trooper to get a feel of what it was like to lug about 50 pounds of gear on a bicycle for four months. As she saw it, her function would be to massage the legs and ego of this man who was abandoning her for a summer as he pursued a dream to travel and write. He promised to call weekly. She promised to send packages. He promised to fly her out sometime during the summer. She said you got that right buddy.

There was no parade that morning. There wasn't a band or display of fireworks. Who knows what morning commuters thought as they saw a man on a purple mountain bike riding along the road that spring.

One moment the bike was stationary. The next it was moving, and the journey had begun.

It is approximately 4,600 miles from Portland to Fairbanks, Alaska. To get there, the route passes through the rolling hills of western Maine and into the White Mountains of New Hampshire. Vermont is the next state before leaving New England and entering New York. The Empire State leads to the Great White North. The plan was to enter Canada at Cornwall, Ontario and head near the nation's capital, Ottawa. Route 17 leads west across the country's never-ending province to North Bay. There the road forks, with both branches ending up in Thunder Bay. At Thunder Bay, another high road-low road scenario exists. Experience has taught that conversations with locals are the best way to decide which way to go.

The next province is Manitoba where the flat, open, windswept plains and West begin. The road heads for Winnipeg. Nearby is the beginning of the Yellowhead Highway which will lead to Saskatoon, Saskatchewan. From there the city hockey great Wayne Gretsky made famous calls — Edmonton, Alberta.

The north by northwest route continues into hardy British Columbia and the Canadian Rockies. The growing community of Dawson Creek is the Mile 0 mark of the Alaska Highway that winds for 1,520 miles to Fairbanks, Alaska. Depending on my physical and mental condition at that point, I would continue to the Pacific Ocean or call it quits.

To get there, I was relying on a 21-speed, purple Novara mountain bike manufactured by REI that had been purchased two years earlier and already had over 3,500 miles on it. It was a touring veteran with experiences through Utah's national parks, Arizona's lonely desert, Mexico's back roads, Colorado's snowy passes and the winds atop New Hampshire's Mount Washington. The logic behind riding a mountain bike versus a road bike was simple: You can go anywhere on a moun-tain bike. You can't on a thin-tired road bike.

The bike was outfitted with front and rear racks. On each rack hung two saddlebags or panniers. There was a handlebar bag, too. Three wa-ter bottles and a pump were carried on the frame.

Tools went in a small bag that fit underneath the seat. Inside was a flat repair kit, allen wrenches, lubricant, spoke wrench, chain link tool, adjustable wrench, bottom bracket tool, clamps and spare screws. A spare tube was stuffed elsewhere. Extra spokes were wrapped with tape on the frame.

Not that I knew what to do with all these tools. I had no idea. Yes, I could fix flats and lubricate chains. I knew enough to find a bike shop every 1500 miles and go in for a tune-up. If one of the screws on a rack would loosen, I could tighten it with an allen wrench. But I am not a fan of hardware stores. The sight of a power tool makes me want to run the other way. I have a philosophy — carry the tool and find someone who knows what to do with it.

Next came clothing. It's best not to take anything you really like. After wearing the same shorts, socks and t-shirts for three or four days without a shower over the course of a summer, it's likely you'll want to burn them at the end of a trip. I took two oh-so-tight riding shorts, one pair of long riding tights, one pair of shorts, one pair of underwear (real cyclists don't wear underwear under there), two pairs of cotton socks, one pair of wool socks, pocketed sweat pants, one polypropylene long sleeve shirt, a riding shirt, a t-shirt, fleece pullover, waterproof shell, wind pants, two bandannas, gloves, overmitts, wool hat, sport sandals, sneakers, a helmet, riding gloves and a baseball cap that had "Alaska" written on the front so I wouldn't forget where I was going. Clothing was rolled and squashed into the rear panniers.

Eighty-five percent of the time I expected to be camping. Tent, sleeping bag and sleeping pad were affixed with two bungie cords to the rear rack. The kitchen was in a front saddlebag. It contained a collapsible stove, fuel and fuel bottle, mess kit, silverware, Swiss Army knife, scrub pad, plastic trash bags, candle lantern, candles, waterproof matches, lighters and flashlight.

The other front bag had toiletries and room for food that would be purchased along the way.

Water purification tablets and a first aid kit also came along for the ride. A camera, several rolls of film, extra batteries, maps, spare bungie cords, portable radio and small tape recorder went too. A wallet and deck of cards were handy. The camera, baseball cap, wallet, map of the day and sunglasses traveled in the handlebar bag.

The Apple PowerBook computer took up one entire saddlebag and weighed nearly 10 pounds with case, pens, business cards specially printed for the trip, modem cord, dry bag and spare disks. Taking a computer opened a new avenue of travel. Through it, I could communicate. Loneliness can become a dark side of touring if you let it get to you. You spend so much time by yourself. Through the computer, I could make friends along the information highway. They would be with me as I cycled through cyberspace. It would be easy for them to find me. They would just type in my screen name, Rodeman, and send it to my electronic mail address. They would be in an office all warm and dry while I was out on the road trying to keep my mouth shut so mosquitoes wouldn't get in. I'd also be getting the tan of a lifetime.

The computer also served as a journal, ledger, office, address book, amusement center and conversation piece. It also forced me to take showers. In order to file stories, I would have to check into a hotel once a week to use the telephone. I was optimistic that I would be able to find one.

The weekly columns were going to four places — *The Conway (N.H.) Daily Sun, The Nashua (N.H.) Telegraph, The Fairbanks (Ak.) News-Miner* and America Online's BikeNet.

I'm a journalist. The career had been okay and included a stint in the Middle East covering the Palestinian uprising and a few Associated Press awards. But the joy of covering news waned quickly. I turned to writing about the outdoors and travel. The more I wrote about it, the more I wanted to be out doing it. That's why with no wife, kids, mortgage or debt I was able to tell the powers that be at *The Conway Daily Sun*, a small New Hampshire daily newspaper where I was employed full-time, it was time for a Maine to Alaska bike trip.

They were supportive and welcomed weekly columns. Upon my return, I could go back, albeit on a part-time basis.

Skiing is also a passion of mine. During the winter months, I was writing ski columns for *The Nashua Telegraph*. Told of the ride, *The Telegraph* signed on too. Hoping to garner a few more newspapers to help underwrite the cost of this $20 a day venture plus film and developing costs, airfare home and phone calls, I queried five other newspapers. *The Fairbanks News-Miner* in Alaska said yes.

Everyone, it seems, has the Alaskan dream. At least once, they need to head to the land of grizzly bears, caribou, gigantic salmon and $2 cans of tuna. My spin to the Alaska paper was, "Let's follow this dream."

When the *News-Miner* bought it, I didn't know that Fairbanks was a hardcore bicycling community because of a university, pleasant bike path network, military bases and a silly, macho race called the Iditasport where entrants pedal for 160 miles through snow and ice in 20-below temperatures.

Finding BikeNet was an accident. Just a few weeks before the trip, a colleague had conned me into trying America Online by having free software sent to my post office mailbox. I tried it. I liked it. Surfing through the web of online information, I stumbled across BikeNet, a forum for bicycle enthusiasts. In what seemed like cyberseconds, a deal was cut — columns for computer time.

Now came the time to name the column, and subsequently, the trip. I had done this for previous cycling adventures. For example, a friend and I once attempted to bicycle from California to New York during the summer following high school graduation. Being arrogant and optimistic 17-year-olds, we had a $1 bet to see who could get laid more often. We dubbed this adventure "The Ride."

"The Ride" busted outside Toronto in a scoreless tie.

Suggestions for this adventure were plentiful. "The Great Ride North," "North Bike Northwest" and "On The Road" were some of the names on the menu. They all came in second to "Against The Wind."

And on that first day from Portland, I knew quickly the name was unfortunately appropriate. I was going the wrong way. The prevailing winds flow from west to east. On that first day, they weren't flowing, but blowing right in my face.

The highest wind gust ever recorded by man on Earth was tabulated atop Mount Washington in New Hampshire. On that day, the wind blew at 231 miles per hour. Mount Washington is also the highest peak in the Northeast. It can be a windy place. The mountain would soon come into view. The foothills waited. The wind howled. My hands grew numb. The butt ached. To assuage the pain, I would dismount every five miles for a stretch and confidence building session with the girlfriend. I would shake out my hands for better circulation.

"You're doing fine. It's not a race. Take your time," the girlfriend would say.

"Who's idea was this?," I would ask.

The girlfriend would give a murderous stare.

Of course, it was my idea. But I hadn't exactly trained hard for this mission. There had been skiing over the winter. Lots of it. There had been some bicycle riding in April, a precarious month in northern New England when rain, sun and snow compete for attention. Rain had won and forced me to the doctor who prescribed penicillin up to three days before lift-off. The best training for this trip had not been physical or mental. It was verbal. I told everyone I knew I was doing it. Therefore I had to do it.

The sea was a memory as Route 25 gave way to 113. The rolling hills of rural western Maine wind past cemeteries, stone walls and 18th century homes. Pick-up trucks were operated by plaid-shirt wearing drivers.

Forty five miles was the goal the first day out. There was a campground in Brownfield where I was looking forward to setting up camp, taking a shower and enjoying a hot meal with my honey.

It was closed, not yet open for the season.

Dejection set in. How could someone who sent away for a dozen maps and campground guides, who spent hours pouring over them, not know about this?

He forgot to call.

Jan saved me.

"I have a friend who lives a few miles from here. I'll call him," she said.

The call was quick.

"Let's go. He lives about two miles that way," she told me, pointing west on a backroad. "His house is just up the hill."

"Up the hill!" screamed the ungrateful, exhausted, Jacuzzi-longing, jelly-legged adventurer. "Up the hill. My legs are toast. My butt's flambe. Why does he have to live up the hill? Don't you know anyone nearby who lives down a hill?"

The stare.

I shut up.

She drove.

I followed up the steep, lumpy, grotesque dirt road to Bill Murphy's home on Burnt Meadow Mountain. By the time I got there, Jan had already settled in and briefed Murphy about my trip.

Murphy was a thin, active sixty-something Mainer who had built his three-level home in 1986. He still worked out, hiked, biked and skied. The man with a blue bandanna wrapped around his long, gray hair to keep it away from his face imparted these words of wisdom to me within 20 minutes of our meeting: "Don't look at the whole thing. Just take the trip one day at a time."

For a Maine to Alaska bike ride, those are words to live by.

A Man and Somebody Else's Dog

E arly morning's are ripe with wildlife for the bicycle rider not afraid of spring frost. A moose was the first sign of predawn life in Crawford Notch, New Hampshire. Bleary eyed, I wasn't sure if it was a sign saying, "Brake for Moose," or the real thing. When I applied my squeaky brakes, the creature trailed off into the woods.

Near Danville, Vermont , a flurry of white-tailed deer startled me before 6 a.m. as I rode along one morning. I think I counted six before they danced away and disappeared. But neither moose or deer could prepare me for "Whitey."

Dogs can terrorize bicyclists. As weapons, riders have used water bottles filled with water, water bottles laced with ammonia, and air pumps. Dogs chained or fenced are great. Pooches that know the property boundary lines and don't cross them are smart. Those that chase cyclists are dumb. And then there's Whitey.

Whitey — that's what I called him since we were never formally introduced — befriended me at a Swanton, Vermont campsite on the banks of Lake Champlain bordering Quebec, Canada on the sixth morning of the ride. The lean, white, boxer with a collar watched as I packed away my gear and looked at me with cute, doggy, give-me-some-food eyes as I wolfed down breakfast. I welcomed the company since that time of year, May 7, not too many folks are touring, let alone camping.

Whitey listened to my stories well.

As I tried to say good-bye, Whitey followed me down Campbell's Bay Road exiting the campground with me. He developed a keen interest in my left shoe as it revolved with the pedals. Whitey tried to take a chunk out of it.

"No," echoed through the chill and quiet.

Whitey obeyed and ran by my side.

"Good dog."

Then he eyed my front tire.

"No. Now go home."

Whitey first tried to taste a piece of rubber. Problem was, he couldn't kill it. The canine had a great deal of trouble sinking his teeth into a moving tire. After a few attempts, he stopped trying.

But Whitey didn't go home.

As the farms and cows rolled by, Whitey met up with a cream-colored friend and the two chased each other under wire fences, playing. They darted all over the road and looked as though they knew the terrain well. They went at it until the rural road ended for the more-traveled Route 2 and Whitey's friend went home.

But Whitey didn't go home.

I hung a right. So did Whitey.

The odometer rolled to two, then three and four. Whitey was still behind me. Up ahead was a bridge.

"Go home."

Maybe Whitey was deaf. He could have just been stupid. Perhaps Whitey didn't speak English. I yelled out "go home" in Spanish.

Still, Whitey didn't go home.

The Yankee fishermen must have been startled from their Saturday angling in Lake Champlain when they saw a man on a fully-loaded bicycle being chased by a boxer over a bridge in northern New England.

The shoulder narrowed and the dog was in serious danger. Whitey was following by my side. Cars stopped. He was nearly hit. Yet the dog wouldn't go. Even a kick did no good.

The odometer tallied five and upstate New York crept closer.

"How long you gonna run your dog?," a voice called out.

"It's not my dog," I said, well aware of a similar scene in the film "The Pink Panther." I don't know if he bites, I thought, but didn't say.

The voice came from a border policeman in his cruiser on the other side of the road. Whitey and I crossed.

"He's been following you for a while," said the officer.

I nodded and explained.

He turned to the dog.

"Do you want to go back to Campbell's Bay Road?"

Before the dog could answer, he looked at the human.

"Open the back door and see if he goes in."

He did, after I pulled him in by the collar.

"Thanks," I said to the officer with the dark sunglasses.

Off went Whitey, the cop and the car.

Whitey finally went home.

Whitey was one of the few companions I had on the road during the first week in May. Before green returns to New England, brown is king. It can be a dismal time. Frost sits on the bicycle seat in the morning. Nights are spent sleeping with a wool cap on. Fleece gloves keep the fingers warm and tights protect the legs in the early morning hours.

There was still a lull in activity as winter sort of ended and spring hadn't yet begun. The signs weren't up yet welcoming visitors to places like the campground in New Hampshire's Crawford Notch State Park or identifying the frigid, snow-fed waterfalls in the mountain pass. There were still patches of snow at the top of the ski areas, but no skiers were schussing down since the resorts were closed.

I was up early, on the road by 6 a.m., partly due to a lack of confidence. My muscles hurt. I wasn't used to carrying the load of my bicycle. I wanted to make sure there was enough daylight to go the 50 miles a day I had projected.

Maine led to New Hampshire and on the second day, I was home again. How strange it is to a be a tourist in your own town, I thought. There was the bike shop in North Conway that tuned the bike just a few days before. Over there was where I went grocery shopping. That's where my hair is cut. There's my favorite bar. Wow, there's the road that leads to Jan's house. Is she home? Hey, that's my post office across from one of the more picturesque vistas of a snow-capped Mount Washington. Wait a minute. There's my condo with a deck overlooking a pool and the views of the Moat mountains. Oh, that's right. I'm here on my bike, pedaling past it on the way to Alaska. Plus, I don't live there anymore. I gave it up and stored my stuff at Jan's.

People often don't take advantage of their own backyard and I was no exception. It had taken me over three years to finally hike the Moats.

I had been in New Hampshire more than five years before climbing Mount Washington. Heck, I grew up in New York and still haven't been to the Statue of Liberty.

So it was with aching lower limbs that I began an ascent I had been avoiding for years — the hilly, slithering crawl through the White Mountain National Forest to Crawford Notch. In truth, the notch isn't really all that difficult. It crests at about 2,000 feet above sea level which is a 1700 foot climb from North Conway. This was tame compared to what waited ahead. However, the timing was bad as the body was not yet lean and mean.

Jan decided to drive ahead to a parking area on the other side of the notch and set up a congratulatory tailgate hot meal for the rider upon the successful completion of this arduous endeavor. She honked and waved before driving off, leaving me alone to start my machine.

The legs started to spin. The hands gripped the handlebar hard. Head down, the traveler progressed. Maybe he began in the highest gear of the second chain ring. The hill got higher, the left thumb shifted the gears on the rear cog lower. The muscles pumped. Sweat made its way through the pores on the forehead and back. Soon the left thumb pressed the lever to drop the chain from the middle to low ring. Energy was expelled. The wheels spun slower. The sweat flowed faster.

I exerted force in the toe clips, awakening new muscle groups that would soon protest, loudly. Slowly I climbed, revolution by revolution. The right thumbed dropped the chain lower and lower. I was now in what seasoned riders call "granny gear." This is when you, in effect, sit and spin up a hill. It is the lowest gear.

What?! The lowest gear! The brain hadn't registered this fact when the thumb clicked the gear and nothing happened. The resistance was the same. I tried again. Nothing happened. The bicycle came to a standstill.

I got off and walked.

There is no shame in dismounting. Walking is a part of bicycle travel. It stretches the muscles and gives the cyclist a breather. The back and neck can feel refreshed in a new position.

At least that's how I rationalized it. That is, until I knew the top was near and Jan would be on the other side.

I got back on.

"Congratulations," she said with a hug. Quite the culinary overachiever, Jan had cooked from a portable stove in the back of her Trooper and had already set up two lawn chairs for the al fresco experience.

What's a guy to do? There was the smile, the aroma, a warm hug.

"Um. I sort of got off the bike and, like, you know, well, boy how about those Red Sox, walked."

"That's okay. You still did it."

How can you not love that? She was right.

So I learned a lesson that day: On the road, there's no hill I can't walk up.

Roadside Dreaming

"Where do you sleep?" is one of the most-often asked questions of a bicycling adventurer. The tent, sleeping bag and pad on the rear of the rig usually give the answer away, but there are times a more direct answer is needed. Campgrounds are the clear choice. They are cheapest which is important to someone traveling by bicycle. After all, if money wasn't an issue don't you think they would fly to their destination? After camping, cyclists choose from hostels, hotels, motels, inn's, bed and breakfast's and strangers' floors.

Sometimes the aforementioned lodging establishments aren't available. Travelers can then head to the local police department, town hall, post office or church and either be invited in or told of a place nearby to camp like a small park that really doesn't allow camping but no one cares if you stay there or not.

Of course, there are times there appears to be nothing around at the end of the day. Sometimes nothing can be something. For instance, a national forest is a legal place for people to camp if they abide by certain rules like pitching a tent away from a trail or so many feet from a water source. Land under the eyes of the Bureau of Land Management is also gratis.

When there clearly is nothing, cyclists have no choice but to stay by the side of the road. Chances are, they are trespassing and it is illegal.

But hey, it's free. It's also scary.

The first time I ever camped by the side of the road was in Mexico during the winter of 1992. Jonathan Winter, a then 27-year-old emergency medical technician and student from the San Francisco Bay area, and I were cycling from Tucson, Arizona to Los Mochis to catch a train through that country's Grand Canyon — the Copper Canyon. Roadside services in northern Mexico aren't as developed as in North America. Tired after a 60 mile day, we were nowhere and the closest somewhere was too far at that point. We opted to pull over and camp.

"You choose the spot," said Jonathan.

We rode on. Each cactus looked the same. There didn't seem to be one place that was more enticing than the other. Jonathan recognized my indecisiveness and announced in an authoritative manner, "Over there."

"Over there" on one side of the road looked no different from "over there" on the other side of the road.

We surveyed the spot. It had dense desert growth which meant we wouldn't' be seen from the road. It was level. There didn't appear to be a water source, but that was okay since our water bottles were topped off.

"Good choice," I said.

Then we set about scaling the barbed-wire fence.

Jonathan went over first. Piece by piece, the equipment and bicycles made it over too. We sidestepped the cow patties and set up. We dared not use the tent because it might attract attention and decided to sleep under the stars. The stars were radiant that night in the southern sky. The constellations seemed to be three dimensional. Perhaps I even saw a shooting star. I saw lots of sky that night because I couldn't sleep. In the back of my mind, the ghost of Pancho Villa was going to ride through the land, stumble upon us, violate our orifices, slit our gringo throats and be off to rape and plunder elsewhere.

How silly I had been. Those thoughts of Mexico were with me as I gazed up at the Vermont sky through the thick woods somewhere along the side of the road near Danville. I had cycled alone over the Connecticut River to Vermont after leaving Jan in New Hampshire. She had to drive back to North Conway and the real world.

Perhaps it was the emotion or the long, steep rolling hills of Route 18, but pretty soon I was drained. Yet something pushed me. It happens sometimes on a bike. You just want to go a few miles more although logic dictates you find a place to stay as you cycle through St. Johnsbury because it's a city and accommodations are readily available. The city becomes a blur and you just go on.

Well pretty soon there was a detour and the next thing I knew I was on a country road heading for a town called North Danville. There wasn't much there except for a church and even with the experience of knowing I could probably stay there, I pressed on, thinking there would be something around the next corner or over the next hill and the only thing that was there turned out to be another corner and another hill.

A woman materialized on the front of her lawn and walked out to her mailbox.

"Is there a place like a campground or hotel in Danville?," I asked.

"No," she said and suggested St. Johnsbury. One no-no of long distance biking seems to be turning back after you're more than a few miles from a point. Once you hit that point of no return, forward is the only direction you can go. I was past the point.

Tired, deflated, I crested one more hill and started looking for a spot. Over there looked good.

Down the rise and into the woods I went. I dared not set up a tent because it would attract attention. I kept low and quiet. I watched joggers go by as evening set in. Cooking was out of the question as the flame and hiss of the stove might be taken for front page news in this part of the world. Dinner was two cans of cold beans.

Darkness came. My lone companion was talk radio. It made me forget where I was.

And as I fell asleep that night, a thought struck me. Soon I would be entering New York. Hadn't the Headless Horseman called New York home?

The far reaches of upstate New York are home to farms, tacky lawn ornaments, Indian Reservations and prisons. It's also where a friend lived, and now on the cusp of having pedaled nearly 300 miles, it was time to telephone a familiar voice and be inside for a night or two, not too far from a microwave, television and VCR. I wanted to practice a little channel-surfing instead of bike riding for a change.

Jeff Jones worked at the Levi's outlet at the Miromar Factory Outlet Center where Canadians, during times of great economic joy, would drive down from the land of taxation and spend their colorful money at rapid rates. These were not prosperous times for our friends in the North. The Canadian dollar was down and talk of Quebec secession spread through the airwaves, making foreign investors look elsewhere.

However, it was a good time to be visiting Canada. After crossing the boarder, everything would be 34 percent off for greenback carriers. The whole country was on sale!

I was carrying a few telephone numbers and addresses with me of people I knew along the way. Jeff was one of them. Being in retail, he worked most weekends and that's what he was doing when I called the store on a late Saturday morning.

"Swing by the store," he said on the other end of the phone. "It's just down the road."

He was right. Minutes later, there was Jeff. Then there I was being introduced to the employees as his stepbrother's friend slash brother's ex-housemate who was riding to Alaska and always does this kind of stuff. Jeff said I would be staying a day or so. We left and he showed me where he lived. Then he went back to work.

Jeff's home was neat for a single guy, and decorated in baseball memorabilia. He showed me where the shower was, told me to make myself home and then went back to work.

A roof felt good. Carpet underneath bare feet was welcomed after a week in a tent. There was even some food in the refrigerator. Not much though. He was single and hard-working which meant fast food was on the menu often. No complaints. Pizza tastes better than cans of cold beans any day. So I picked up the remote, found my position on the couch and didn't move until Monday morning.

Ontario

Welcome to the Great White North

"**A**re you carrying any tobacco?," asked the woman in the booth at the border.

"No, ma'am."

"What about alcohol?," she inquired.

"No, ma'am."

"Firearms?"

"No."

"Citizenship."

"United States."

"How long do you expect to be in Canada?"

"As long as it takes me to ride through it."

"Go ahead."

That was it. I wasn't asked for identification. No one wanted to go through my bags. I didn't need a passport. The collector on the American side didn't even want the fee. He let me keep the $2.25 toll and said to go around the wire that keeps count of the number of vehicles going across the Seaway International Bridge which spans the St. Lawrence River into Cornwall, Ontario from upstate New York.

I wasn't alone as I crossed into the Great White North on May 10, 1994. The day before, Jan had returned in her Trooper for two days of accompaniment. She had brought along a mutual friend named Henry Sirois. Sirois loved the outdoors, parties and people. In his 50's, Henry had more hair than a man of his age should be allowed. He had made millions in the leather industry and lost it. His current occupation was ski instructor and masseuse. An avid cyclist, he wanted to see what long-distance bicycle travel was like without actually having to carry all the stuff that goes with it.

We had arranged to meet along Route 11 in New York. They knew I had stayed at Jeff Jones', so they plotted how far they thought I could pedal in their drive from New Hampshire. On a hill outside of Chateauguy, the familiar beige vehicle pulled over and out came the biggest smile I had seen in days — Jan's.

"We figured you would be around here," said Henry as he exited the vehicle during a roadside hug session.

Henry would ride with me by bike. Jan would follow along by car. This might not seem fair at first, but it was. Jan is crafty. She makes baskets, jams, pies, cookies, knits, sews and does all those things that people under 60 aren't supposed to do because they're too busy making a living. Yes, there was joy in seeing her honey, but there was also joy in searching for weeds.

Jan had a reputation as a weed hunter. During road trips, she would pull over from the road as she spotted a patch. The passenger would then roll his or her eyes, knowing that soon this energetic pistol would pop out of the car with the clippers she always carried and begin snipping away. This trip was no different.

"Did she do the weed thing?," Henry was asked.

He rolled his eyes.

Henry got his bicycle off the rack and we agreed to meet in Malone some 10 miles down the road for lunch. Having ridden with no one for a week, Henry's presence was appreciated. He clicked on his little radio that he carried in a handlebar bag and we listened to a station in French as the border got closer. We got to Malone before Jan did. When she finally got there, an explanation wasn't necessary. Henry and I looked at each other and smiled after helping get the food out of the rear of the vehicle. To get to the bags, we had to sift through the weeds.

Hail is not popular with cyclists. Put on a bicycle helmet and have a friend dump a tub full of ice cubes on your head. You'll have an idea of how it feels to be out riding when the clouds darken, the wind howls, and grape-sized chunks of ice start dropping from the sky.

The hail stings the unprotected extremities. The frozen balls stick and collect around hairy legs, forming a chilling layer of icing on the rider. Or if the rider is wearing black tights, it splotches the material with white. The face is a favorite target. It's as if thousands of needles are pricking the skin. A person can get sick quickly. Finding shelter immediately is advisable.

The sky appeared menacing over Route 2 along the St. Lawrence River. A dark front was ahead and it would be a matter of minutes before Henry and I would be directly underneath. In times of bad weather, I would stop to get a few of the trash bags out to wrap my tent, sleeping bag and sleeping pad. Most of the items inside the panniers were in plastic bags, too, so I wasn't too concerned about anything getting wet. We stopped and prepared.

Being two stubborn males, it didn't occur to us to rest somewhere and let the storm pass. There was a false security in our psyches that said Jan would be by in the event of foul weather to rescue us from the impending downpour.

The temperature shot down quickly as the wind picked up. Hail started to fall, bouncing around like marbles. The headlights of cars shone brighter in the darkness. Inside the comfort of a warm automobile, drivers could keep one hand on the wheel while the other hand flicked on the windshield wipers with nary a care.

"Poor suckers," some must have thought seeing the two wet cyclists trudging on through the onslaught.

Shelter didn't appear right away. No, that would have made things too easy. Time was needed to let the weather creep into the clothes and make riding uncomfortable. The water didn't seep into the upper body. The shell I was wearing was an excellent piece of equipment for protecting against the elements.

The tights were starting to dampen, but body heat from my legs kept me warm. It was the squishing in the sneakers that made us squint harder through the hail to find a place out of nature's way. Where the first droplets of moisture enter the sneaker, I don't know. Maybe some sneak their way in through the tiny ventilation holes. Some just hitch a ride down on the tights, changing form from hail to liquid, following the grooves to the ankle. There's room between the laces and eyelets for a few buggers to slide in. Once they're on the inside, they drop down on the tongue and make their way along to the sock where they all accumulate and begin chomping on the skin to make it cold, clammy and squishy.

Between the soaked sneakers and pedaling it was as if my feet were on a seesaw in a swimming pool. Each revolution, the water would go from the front of the shoe to the back, giving both toes and heels a respite before being dunked again.

Henry was several hundred yards ahead of me. That wasn't hard considering I was carrying 50 pounds of stuff to his nothing. I saw him start to make a left turn.

Now it was like riding in the bottom of a draining bathtub. The water from the road parted to make way for the tires. Not only was the hail soaking me, but I was also hit by the spray from my own wheels and those from the passing cars.

Henry had dismounted and was standing under a toll booth for the Long Sault Parkway, a road that juts into the St. Lawrence. The hail was still falling and we almost had to shout to hear each other as it echoed from the overhang. We had found shelter. Now we had to stay warm.

While riding, our bodies produced heat. Now inactive, we had to put on more layers while taking off the dripping clothing. Henry sat on the curb to take off his riding shoes and leaned against the booth door. He nearly fell backward as the door opened to a freshly painted, heated room.

Inside, we took off our sneakers, socks, helmets, shells, riding gloves and tights and draped them over the heaters. Clearly, this booth was being readied for the approaching Victoria Day weekend, Canada's Memorial Day, and the unofficial start of summer which was hard to believe since it looked like winter wasn't ready to give up yet. The provincial park employees were cleaning it up.

Rest, warmth and a few snacks such as trail mix passed the time as the hail soon abated. Talk then centered on catching up with Jan.

"She'll find us," said Henry.

"Yup."

From the window we could see Route 2. We could also see the Trooper with New Hampshire plates pass by. Minutes later, a security guard showed up. He was very curt, even rude and demanded we get the hell out of there immediately. Henry isn't one to be spoken to rudely. So when the opening salvo is fired, take cover.

"You know I can bring you up on trespassing charges," the grumpy man said with a scowl.

"Go ahead and do that. The door was open. We were getting out of the storm."

"I don't care what you were doing. Just get out of here."

"Thanks for the welcome to Canada buddy. You're one helluva good-will ambassador."

That ended the exchange as Henry and I gathered our things. Mr. Grump watched over us and slammed the door extra hard for our benefit as we left. He walked back to his car, opened the door and pointed his finger at us, but then thought about it and got in without saying a word.

He drove away.

What a jerk, was the consensus between Henry and me. With the storm gone and blue skies on the way, we put on our tainted items and started to ride. Fairly soon the Trooper came at us, made a U-turn and out popped Jan.

"I was trying to figure out where you guys would be," she said.

"You passed us over there," I said.

"Did you get wet?," she asked. "There was plenty of sunshine a mile down the road. I got a lot of baskets done."

The eyes rolled.

We spent the night about three miles up the road in a hotel with the heat cranked up to over 80 degrees Fahrenheit to dry our clothes.

Jan and Henry's visit was much too short, I thought as the road continued north without them. Tearful good-byes aren't much fun either. I wouldn't see Jan again for another six weeks, but telephone contact kept us together at least once a week.

Early May in northern Ontario can be a time for isolation or introspection. It is also a time when campgrounds haven't opened yet. Provincial workers are starting to turn on the water, paint the picnic tables and do some yard work, but the grounds aren't open to the public. That's good news for bicyclists. The joy of traveling by bike is that you go around or under an obstacle in the road. Since you don't make much noise, chances are no one will hear you. Keep quiet and don't build a fire. If a worker stumbles upon you, chances are they'll let you stay. If not, just pedal away and come back. There aren't many travelers out during midweek as cars carry commuters to work. That changes on Fridays.

Canadians are mad about canoes. On Fridays, just watch the procession northward as canoes and kayaks adorn the rooftops for weekend paddles. After all, the country was founded by paddlers.

As Canadians are quick to point out, their country is not part of the United States. Once over the boarder, the currency changes. Gone were America's drab green bills. Instead, colorful currency rested in my wallet until it was time to change hands. A dollar coin worked well here. Canadians seemed to love them. They called them "loonies" in honor of the bird that graces its face. Gasoline is sold in liters. If a resident of a town is in the National Hockey League, a sign declares so at the entrance to the community. Pedaling was now done in kilometers as the metric system is used in Canada. English and French are the official languages so official signs carry both languages. There were pockets where the French inflection seemed predominant. Others, hints of the Crown could be heard in the voices. The further west one travels in Canada, the less French is seen and heard. Also, it was odd getting distances from merchants, restaurant workers and gas station employees. Some answered in miles while the rest preferred to click off in kilometers.

It was too early to head into a city. The road led to the nation's capital, Ottawa, on the banks of the Ottawa River. No doubt the city would be a fascinating place for culture, cuisine and a shower. However, entering a major metropolitan area on a bicycle can be a confusing, exhausting experience. Roads on a map can be deceiving. The map doesn't tell you about the stop lights and the urban sprawl of fast food stores, discount shops and malls. The lines don't tell you about the accelerated pace of life. One way streets and roads that don't allow bicycles aren't evident. How easy it is to spend extra miles and energy searching for an inexpensive accommodation that is probably on the other side of town and in an undesirable neighborhood. The decision to cycle around Ottawa on back roads and link up with the TransCanada Highway was simple.

There was also a shock upon first seeing this cross-Canada route that was going to be my path for many a mile. The quiet was gone. Tranquillity was quickly forgotten as the sounds of civilization roared past at 60 miles per hour. Cars zoomed by. Trucks, big elephants with mighty tusks just waiting to impale me, hogged the road. There were so many of them — 16-wheelers, 24-wheelers, single trucks, double trucks, mail trucks, fuel trucks, logging trucks, food trucks, clothing trucks.

I looked for a shoulder. Instead, there was only gravel. A queasiness filled my stomach. Who planned this damn trip? How could they be so stupid? What the hell are you doing on bicycle at 32-years-old anyway? You should be at work, playing phone tag with the wife and worrying about the mortgage, putting the kids through college and scheduling a free Saturday three weeks in advance!

Narrow shoulders and screaming trucks make for a frightening experience. The wind created by the monstrous vehicle as it breezes by can knock you off the road. Just hearing them approach from behind can psychologically maim a rider and force them off the road. The echoing of their horn, often a courtesy warning to vacate the premises, can be misinterpreted as a death charge if it interrupts a day dream.

As with anything new, there is uncertainty, fear. I was gripped by it. These were monster trucks ready to trample me. I rode. I walked. Somehow I inched my way about 35 miles into Arnprior and took shelter in a hotel. The trucks never left though. Even at night, I could hear them in the distance, waiting with sharp hungry teeth for a bite to eat.

The trucks never did take a bite of me. As the ride progressed, the traffic thinned in between cities. Traffic was also less congested in the early mornings. Still not confident, still wondering if I would get to Alaska before snow enveloped the land, riding began early. The truckers weren't up yet. The road was mine.

In time, even the roar of the trucks became part of the landscape. Honks became hellos. A wave from an approaching trucker took the place of a conversation. Truckers became ideal sources of information. Sure, there was the occasional nuisance. Sadistic drivers would like to sneak up during day dreams and blast their horn. But that didn't happen often.

Cleaning day at the School House Museum in Deep River was scheduled for Saturday, May 14. On that day, members of the Rolph, Buchanan, Wylie and McKay Historical Society set to work dusting, chalking, drilling and hammering the museum that shows how life once was along the Ottawa River.

From trapping and timber in the 1860s, the region now has nuclear power and a hydroelectric dam. The towns of Deep River and Chalk River were settled in the mid-1800s. The mill industry that once sustained the area was replaced in 1945 when the first nuclear reactor outside the United States began operation nearby.

Now sportsmen come to hunt, fish and paddle while logging trucks still run the roads. Hungering for human interaction, the sounds of saws and hammers first alerted the aural senses. Then sight kicked in. There were cars and pick-up trucks on the grass. People scampered into and out from the many buildings that once housed pioneers who had never seen a television, microwave or even a radio. Men were up high on ladders. Top hats, dresses and rugs from the turn of the century sat on a white wooden banister in the sun. A door was open to let spring in.

Even before I entered the museum, the questions started. These folks were friendly. Soon, a cup of coffee was thrust into my hand and an impromptu tour had begun. Inside the museum were samples of kitchenware, clothing, snowshoes, corking machines, the first outboard motor for the area which was dated around 1900, clothing and perhaps most impressive, a birch canoe.

"The canoe is made of birch and tied together with spruce roots. Could you put someone in the woods and expect them to do that today? They wouldn't know how," said a man I would only know as Guy. Such is the case sometimes while traveling by bicycle. Encounters are short. Faces remain nameless. First names don't have last names. But memories of their kindness are lasting.

Guy relayed a tale about one resourceful trapper. This man would make a canoe for each lake he would work. That way, he didn't have to carry it from waterway to waterway. Although much of Canada is linked by water, early portages could be brutal.

One woman came over and told me about the fall lumberjack supper. On the menu that day will be a logger's fare of roast pork, beans and potatoes. The highlight of the meal is dessert, which consists of pies. Pies are serious business in places where there is nothing else for culture, where culture is defined as Broadway, Lincoln Center or a Museum of Fine Arts. Apple pie, blueberry pie and rhubarb pie contests, festivals and community suppers saturate small town North America during harvest season. Deep River was no different. The previous fall, the woman said 147 pies were made. About 1,000 people live in Deep River.

Stay for supper was soon the cry from the volunteers. The welcome was warm, but the invitation denied. Still early in the day, the road called. I could hear hammers pound nails as Alaska whispered through the trees.

Alone again, I soon longed for conversation and wondered why I hadn't stayed. The scent of the road is often too strong to resist.

It's fairly easy to start a conversation in Canada. Bring up fishing, hockey or politics and everybody is talking. If you're not in the conversational spirit, there's always plenty to eavesdrop on in a roadside restaurant. Ten in the morning or so would be a good time to go into a restaurant for coffee and a late breakfast or early lunch. It wasn't necessary for me to speak, just listen.

Sometimes I would go 24 hours without saying a word. When the urge came to interact,I would go into a truck stop. After all, a waitress *has* to talk to you. So do librarians and police officers. They were always a good source of companionship for a few moments. Rest is sometimes forgotten on bike trips too. The desire to get to where it is you are going transcends everything else. For eight straight days and some 400 miles I rode without a break from Champlain, N.Y. to North Bay, Ontario.

The day I was leaving North Bay the travel gods intervened and told me to stop. By 7 a.m. I was on the road. The wind was in my face as the mercury hovered near the 36 degree mark. A massive hill greeted me outside of the city. So did construction and a ripped up road with no shoulder. Commuters were driving to work. The road was clogged, the traffic just inches from me. The hill was wearing me out. So was the cold and the wind. Everything was working against me. The cycling was unbearable. I hated doing what I was doing. It was so cold.

The wind never rested. It ripped into my clothes, tore into my gloves and across my tights. This was the wind ripping across Lake Nipissing. I had made a decision to head north, north to the cold, to a ripping, brutal wind. I had heard this route was flatter than the one that would head into Sault Sainte Marie and along the shores of Lakes Huron and Superior and into Thunder Bay. I had decided to pedal up and into nowhere.

This road to nowhere was defeating me. I didn't want to go on, but I couldn't bear to turn back. I pulled off into the woods and nearly cried. Who's idea was this? How stupid could I be? Why couldn't I be more like everybody else my age — with a wife, a kid and a safe, warm, dry house?

I was exhausted, but kept moving. I walked. I rode. The wind didn't abate. Nor did the cold.

After 12 miles, a hotel appeared. It wasn't even 9 a.m. I checked in and slept most of the day away.

Hotels were spots I would use my computer and modem. Being a cyberspace neophyte, I hadn't learned of the joys of an acoustic coupler. This is a device that attaches from a computer to the mouthpiece of a telephone. This enables the user to accept and transmit data from virtually any telephone, like a pay phone. It is a must for travelers using a computer and modem. I didn't have one. My computer came with a cord that plugged directly from the computer into a telephone jack in the wall. I figured that would be enough to get by.

Wrong.

Many inexpensive hotels do not have phones in the rooms. They have a pay phone in the lobby. That was useless for me. Also, to prevent towel thieves from also making off with the telephones in the room, many hotel rooms don't even have telephone jacks. I didn't make it clear what I wanted a few times when I checked into a hotel. At a North Bay hotel that doubled as an RV park, I had to transmit my story from the laundry room since that was the only place the desk clerk and I could find a jack. I opened up an ironing board, placed the laptop on it and zapped away.

I also started receiving e-mail. The messages came from people with screen names like chickadee, penneyasoc and rettal. Some were colleagues, others were people I had never met before. Once a week, I would try to get online and correspond with my friends in cyberspace. As the trip progressed, Rodeman's e-mail grew. Messages would come from Alaska, New Hampshire, Virginia, Texas, Calgary and Manitoba. One person kept me abreast of New Hampshire news with a weekly update. Others wanted to know how many calories I consumed a day, how I trained for this and whether I had won the lottery or gained a great inheritance to be able to go on a trip of this magnitude. I had inherited nothing, I would answer. I just saved up for the trip.

Some learned of my trip from friends. Others learned through the newspapers as each column contained my e-mail address. Others followed the journey on Bikenet.

As I rode across Canada, I had access to local telephone numbers that put me online. Although that saved on local calls, there was a surcharge that was applied for each minute used that drove the cost up. Also, I found it was sometimes cheaper for me to call a phone number in the United States than use a local number in Canada because of the surcharge, Nonetheless, I grew to look forward to corresponding with my computer friends.

Riding Down Memory Lane

Floyd Dyer is a bit of an adventurer. The Matheson farmer and father of four once rode his bicycle from the Ontario community of Timmins to New York City. He covered the 1,226 miles, leaving on May 17 and returning via hitchhiking, October 17. Dyer did it when he was 20. That was in 1946. He didn't have 21 gears. He had one. Nor did he have hand brakes. They were using coaster brakes back then, nearly a half century ago.

He left with 90 Canadian dollars and got work in the states caddying at a golf course. He hooked up with a fellow cyclist from New Haven, Connecticut who educated Dyer on hostels. The newfound friend also helped Dyer get a new bicycle and put it on the train back to Timmons when Dyer's first machine was stolen in the Bronx. Some things don't change.

Dyer could click off the distances as if he were cycling yesterday. Timmins to Matheson. Matheson to Kirkland Lake. Temagami to North Bay. Except in 1946, the road from Temagami to North Bay was gravel. Today it is paved.

I met Floyd, his wife Ruth, son George and friend Terry in Matheson after they canoed the Black River. A loaded bicycle is a natural conversation piece and the next thing I knew I was on the Dyers' farm, wolfing down steak, potatoes, salad and the best red currant pie this side of the border.

The police had sent me down to the picnic tables at Black River. The rest in North Bay had proved miraculous and I just cycled about 95 miles from Englehart. The thought of going on was defeated by the soreness in my legs. However, there was an inside exhilaration knowing that the body was getting stronger.

Too cheap to look for a hotel, I went to the police station in Matheson to ask the dispatcher if there were any campgrounds in the area. I explained I had passed one coming into town, but it was closed. The nearest campground, she said, was at a nearby provincial park about 20 miles away. That's nearby if you are in a car. By bicycle, at least on that day, it was out of the question.

But the dispatcher was resourceful and suggested I camp down by the Black River in town. To be sure everything would be okay, she told me a cruiser would swing by in the evening to check on me.

Matheson had everything I needed that day — a grocery store and laundry. Washing clothing on the road can sometimes be a challenge. With items so closely wrapped together in a saddlebag, nothing is really ever clean. If you haven't worn something in a few days, it has the illusion of being clean, but stuffed deep in the bag and exposed to the elements, it takes on a road flavor that permeates the cyclist.

Plus, you can't wash everything. Laundry is done in a public place. Therefore, you must wear clothes. Unless you are willing to stand naked while the spin cycle is engaged, you always have something on and it will not be clean. In the heat of summer, many male cyclists strip down to just shorts, sit in the waiting area and read outdated magazines and supermarket tabloids. They don't care. They'll never be passing that way again.

I wanted to get out of the clothing I was wearing. I found some "clean" black sweat pants in the bottom of my bag and a t-shirt I hadn't worn for a while. I looked for the bathroom to change. There wasn't one. This was a cruel joke.

I contemplated doing a quick change right there as the machines spun, but there were a handful of people. Not that they would care. I just couldn't do it. Instead, I went outside and behind the laundry for a quick change, mooning Matheson in the process. After washing clothes, I headed to the river front for a late lunch/early dinner to recharge the human battery.

The boat launch was somewhat busy. Fisherman cast their lines. A few teens were preparing their boat for what looked like an overnight adventure. A family of four went into the boathouse and prepared two canoes for launch. Those were the Dyers and friend. Floyd walked over from the boathouse and peppered me with questions about the number of speeds, gear ratio and water carrying system. He was amused that I carried a sleeping pad. The sight of four saddlebags also put a grin on his face.

"You're carrying too much," he said.

That's when I learned about Floyd's bicycling adventure from Timmins to New York.

I watched as the four paddled out and about. Four bologna sandwiches, a bag of potato chips and some juice were consumed. A newspaper was read.

"You're still here," said Floyd after the paddle. "Have you had dinner?"

"No," I said. The sandwiches were, after all, just appetizers.

"Then follow us home. We're about two miles down the road."

That they were. A long dirt driveway led to the gentleman's farm. I had no misgivings about accepting the invitation. The four foot high cross on the front lawn was a sign that everything would be okay.

The Dyers, particularly Floyd, were interested in seeing my tent. Though the ground was still damp, as the spring thaw still wasn't complete yet, I set it up in front of the brick farmhouse. You could easily spot the visitor. He was the only one without mudboots.

Floyd was quick to inspect it. I had nearly turned around to get my sleeping bag from the bike, when the 70-year-old Floyd was already inside and commenting.

"Lots of room in there. It's a hotel compared to what I had."

It had been years since Floyd had talked about his bicycle trip, and that night, we sat around the table listening to Floyd recount his adventure. The years had not diminished his enthusiasm. If there is something that can bond two people, it is shared adventure. It doesn't have to come in the form of actually traveling together. The sharing of an activity, even if it is 50 years apart, is enough to make explorers kindred spirits. The spirit was thick that night.

Floyd's trip, though shorter, seemed more difficult than the one I was on. He didn't have four saddlebags. He just had a knapsack. In it were long pants. One set of clothing was used for riding. The other set, which included a tie, was used just on Sunday. Floyd didn't want to miss church. Riding helmets probably hadn't been invented yet. There were two speeds at which Floyd could travel. He either rode or walked. Twenty one speeds on a mountain bike seemed nearly incomprehensible to a man who pedaled so far with one.

So did carrying a portable stove. That brought laughs as well. Floyd's roadside fare consisted largely of bread, honey, milk and bacon. He would fry the bacon in the pan he carried on a campfire he would build every night. Campsites with laundry facilities, ping pong tables, video games and vending machines weren't around. On occasion he would stay at a relative's house for a good sleep indoors.

Floyd's reminiscences were cut short by a national event in Canada — a hockey game. This is a true phenomenon in the Great White North. Not only was this a hockey game, but a play-off one at that. The television set went on promptly at 9 p.m. The family gathered. Conversation was confined to the sport. Only during the period breaks could other subjects be talked about, but quickly. Apparently Canadians actually pay attention to what's being said by the television commentators during a pause in the action.

This was the year in which the New York Rangers, a team from the other side of the border, would win the Stanley Cup. There would be no joy in Canada that season. What joy there was, came from meeting a family who took in a stranger. I never did sleep in the tent that night. Floyd and Ruth insisted I stay inside.

The next morning, with a belly full of bacon and a standing invitation to come back, I cycled down the dirt driveway as the Dyers waved good-bye.

If I hadn't taken the high road — Route 11 — from North Bay, I would not have met the Dyer's and experience their hospitality and friendship. The thought of cycling the Canadian "bush" excited me. Many Ontarians I had met had never been up that way.

This far north, it stays light until 9:30 p.m. or so. Tomatoes don't get planted outside until about June 20th. The rivers and streams flow north into the Arctic Ocean. Pastimes are hunting moose and bear, fishing, nordic skiing and snowmobiling.

The wind can blow hard. It can come at you with persistent jabs until a hook just knocks you out and makes you beg for mercy.

But on those calm days, it's easy to cycle 60 miles, find a spot off the road, and head into the bush.

You would think that the water would be pure this far north, about a 10 hour drive from Toronto. In Temagami the municipal water supply had been contaminated by giardia. Residents had been boiling water for a month and buying it in stores.

At a truck stop in Kenogami, people said the salt the highway department had spread in winter, infiltrated the well. They were using bottled water until a new well would be dug.

Also at that truck stop, I met a man from Fairbanks, Alaska. He figured it would take him 10 days to get home. I figured I would get there by the end of August.

Taking so long gave me a chance to observe roadside phenomena. Northern Ontario has a fare share of manmade roadside kitsch on Route 11. This two-lane highway with varying shoulders (from none to not much) was home to a number of rather large, stiff plastic and wooden animals. These mammals weren't dangerous. Actually, they were quite funny and provided both humor and shade because of their location and size.

Dymond, Ontario was home to Ms. Claybelt. The area around her town was a fertile valley. There was farming and many cows. Ms. Claybelt was a giant Holstein cow. She welcomed visitors to the area. I think she smiled as I stopped under her for lunch.

Further down the road was the world's largest sculpted bison. If there was a sign that said the creatures name, I didn't see it. Whether or not he knew Ms. Claybelt, I did not know. But this gigantic creature was outside keeping watch at the entrance of the Northern Frontier Zoo in Earlton.

Cochrane, one of the last outposts of what many might consider civilization, was home to a rather tame looking polar bear. The white beast called the visitor center its home. It stood guard outside the offices where tourists would pick up maps, brochures and a hot cup of coffee on a cool morning. The train dubbed the Polar Bear Express left from Cochrane and chugged up to Moosonee, a Native American town people in New York would probably consider being located on the edge of nowhere.

I wondered how these giant animals got there. Perhaps Noah had transported them via his ark. That was unlikely as Turkey, where it is said the ark now lies, was thousands of miles away and one long walk for these guys. Chances are they were strapped down on one of the many trucks that zoomed by on the road.

But it wasn't until I pedaled into the Ontario town of Moonbeam that I got my answer. There by the side of the road, just down the block

Northern Ontario is home to a fair share of roadside kitsch like a giant cow, bison and polar bear. The flying saucer in Moonbeam, Ontario is another example of interesting monuments in Canada. (Photo by Marty Basch).

from the Blue Moon Hotel, was a flying saucer — the biggest one I had ever seen.

The Better Side of Nowhere

"Oh, you took the cold route," was the welcome from the woman who ran the campground on a drizzly day in Nipigon.

Nipigon, famed for its five to eight pound river trout, is also a crossroads. Here, Routes 11 and 17 meet about 700 miles after leaving North Bay. Route 17 hugs two Great Lakes while 11 goes north. It was best described to me by a trucker. "You'll see plenty of bush and it's flat."

He forgot cold.

On May 25, I got caught in a few snow squalls outside of Mattice. May 26 started with my water bottles frozen solid. I couldn't get drinking water the following day at a camp at Klotz Lake. The line froze overnight.

On days like these, I rode wearing nearly everything I had. Wool socks kept my toes warm while bicycling gloves, topped by fleece gloves followed by overmitts did the same for my hands and fingers. I rode with a wool hat under my helmet. I probably looked stupid, but I was warm. Such is spring in Ontario.

There was plenty of cold, and plenty of flat too. No, this wasn't desert flat where the road goes on forever and ripples in the harsh sun. This was bush flat. There were long, slight hills and lots of straightaways where people lived in farms or in homes to try their hands at mining and logging. Fields were burned for better crops and wood was the ubiquitous necessity of the north, stacked up nearly to a few roofs.

The road, the northern route of the TransCanada Highway and a favorite with truckers, took users by lakes, leafless and lifeless birch and maple trees and tall, thin evergreens. Signs for moose were more frequent than traffic lights. This is what they call the bush here. It's called the woods where I come from.

"Oh there's nothing up there. It's just the middle of nowhere," was the frequent response from people down south before I headed this way. I found the further away you are from a place, the less people know about it.

But if this was nowhere, nothing, I saw the better side of it, and it came in the most unlikely places.

The 130-mile stretch between Hearst and Longlac is arguably the most desolate section of the road. On a map, there's nothing there except five rest areas with picnic tables and toilets. Usually, they are by a stream or lake. There's water, but nothing else.

The further south I was, the more nothing there was. Then, rumbles were made about a gas station or a store or a camp the closer I got to Hearst. At Hearst, I picked up supplies like beans, tuna, sardines, bananas and noodles since I was about to cycle through the northern abyss. I even registered with the police to let them know my plans.

"There's not much between here and Longlac," said a dispatcher.

"So I've heard," I answered as I provided her my driver's license, and she recorded my name, address and birthdate.

Still, I didn't have much choice. I just went on. I was compelled to go. There was no turning back.

Some 10 miles outside of Hearst, I saw a man get out of a truck and stand in front of it. He followed me with a stare as I cycled closer.

"It's me," he said.

I looked again.

"From last night."

"Oh yeah," I said after looking a third time. He owned the campground in Mattice where I had stayed. We chatted about my day and he told me about Mooseland up ahead. I was nowhere and I knew someone.

Mooseland is in the middle of nowhere, or more precisely, at the junction of Routes 11 and 631, 40 miles west of Hearst. It is a service station with gas pumps, a motel and a platter called the Mooselander which consists of two half pound burgers topped with gravy and fried onions. The latter can satisfy any hunger. Cyclists tend to remember these things. When food is your fuel, you often look for the best grade and huge burgers burn exceptionally well. And you can eat these things because what comes in is later exhausted during riding.

The place has been run since 1989 by Tom and Patricia Hamelin. It's a joint that looks profitable, but you have to work at it 17 hours a day and with three kids that can be tough.

"We've only been home for Christmas once in the past five years," said Patricia. They're thinking of selling.

With the motel booked, Patricia let me camp out in a grassy section of the place for free. The next morning I asked if there was anything before Longlac. There was. Patricia said there was their other lodge, a rest area, another home, some camps and the camp at Klotz Lake that had a store. She told me which side of the road they were on and pointed out other landmarks. There were also satellite towers, compressor stations for the TransCanada pipeline, a few outfitters, garbage dumps and gravel roads that went off into nowhere.

Sixty-four miles later I was at Klotz Lake where someone had pulled out a 26-pound pike a few days before I got there. I shopped at the meager store. I took a shower.

I met a guy named Rick who was making boxes out of wood and moose horns and engraving names on them. Rick was a scruffy looking guy in blue jeans, baseball cap and multiple day growth beard on his face.

He seemingly had worked everywhere in Canada from the Baffin Islands to Inuvik, near the Beufort Sea in the Northwest Territories.

"You have to take the Dempster Highway to get there," I said.

Rick had driven it. Said the 400-mile plus road was all gravel.

"Yeah, if you go up there you'll be spending a lot of nights in the bush. There's nothing there," he said.

A Man Named Manfred

For nearly a month, the road had been void of other long-distance bicycle riders. The only travelers were in cars, trucks and vans. That changed on June 1 in Kakabeka Falls Provincial Park, just outside Thunder Bay, Ontario.

Ramen noodles were on the menu. The air was still a bit frosty and the picnic tables had dried from the night's rain.

As the water was boiling, I read *The Chronicle Journal*, the Thunder Bay morning daily newspaper. There wasn't much on the front page. Stories about the railroad, a fine in the death of a miner and the future of the Great Lakes-St.Lawrence Seaway didn't hold much interest. Neither did the color photos showing the change in the Thunder Bay police uniforms. The city's finest would be outfitted in a navy shirt, replacing the more subdued baby blue version.

There was one story though I had to read.

It was about me.

"North to Alaska, by bicycle" said the headlines. The subhead, which is the type under the headline, read "Cyclist says our 'Courage Highway' is aptly named."

There on page one was a color photo of yours truly, seated on the bicycle seat and typing on the keyboard of the computer. The photo had been staged the day before in the entrance to the newspaper, near the waters of Lake Superior. I must admit, I contacted the newspaper to do the story. Now getting stronger, I felt I had the confidence to tell my story. This was part ego and part education. The ego wanted a souvenir from Ontario. This article would be it. The lesson would be to encourage people to take a risk, follow a dream, get off your duff and do something.

Seeing oneself in the paper is a strange experience — especially if you are used to being on the other side of the story. Reading words you supposedly said the day before is even stranger. The worst though, is reading words you didn't say and spotting glaring errors.

Here was the story:

> After dodging trucks on the Terry Fox Courage Highway, cyclist Marty Basch thinks he knows how it got its name.

> "Between Nipigon and Dorion, (there are) no shoulders, said the 32 year old New Hampshire journalist. "You have to have courage to do it."

> For Basch — bicycling between Portland, Maine and Fairbanks, Alaska — that stretch of Highway 11-17 is just one of the many roads he's tackled since leaving Maine May 2.

> "Everybody has a dream," he said Tuesday, looking remarkably fresh for someone who had ridden about 2,200 kilometres in the last month. "I've always used the bicycle as a means of travel."

> Basch managed to swing a four-month sabbatical from work to do the journey, getting paid only for the stories he writes.

> He doesn't know if he'll be able to claim the mileage as a business expense.

> A seasoned veteran of long cycling trips, Basch comes well-equipped to handle any challenge. His 22-gear mountain bike is saddled with about 55 pounds of camping gear, clothing, food and — essential for roving reporters — a portable computer.

> Basch uses his high-tech tool to files stories on his journey to three newspapers as well as to the international computer network Internet.

> Each night he enters his mileage, aches, pains and observations in his diary on his computer, outfitted with a telephone modem and the latest software.

> His entries tell of the people and places he sees on

his journey, including Nipigon where he said he was clothed in his winter woolies during the cold spell last week.

"Such is spring in Northern Ontario," he wrote.

Although Basch's route along northern Highway 11 was flatter than the more scenic, but physically draining Highway 17, he still ran into his share of difficult terrain which didn't slow him down at all.

"I have no problem walking up hills."

Basch's bike stirred up some fond memories for a 70 year old man he met in Matheson, near Timmins. The older man had taken a similar trip in 1946 from Timmins to New York on a one-speed.

"He also got his bicycle stolen in the Bronx," laughed Basch. "Some things haven't changed that much."

Sure, the story left a smile across my face, thinking about Floyd Dyer and the other places I had just been. But soon, I also felt a bit betrayed by the potholes in the story. There were two outstanding errors. First, my bike had 21 gears, not 22. Second, my stories weren't filed on the Internet, but America Online.

So I picked nits. There wasn't much else for me to do as the water boiled for the noodles. Also, I never said there were no shoulders on the Fox Highway. I said there were *virtually* no shoulders. There's a difference.

Without a dinner partner, my complaints about the story were only heard by the trees, picnic tables and wind.

That is, until three accented words cut through the spring.

"Zere you are."

The words woke me from my soliloquy.

"I been looking for you."

Whoever this was had found me. He looked happy. After I looked at him, so was I.

It was a fellow traveling cyclist, the first I had run into since the journey began.

What an odd man this was. His huge, Dumbo-like ears stuck out like wings from beneath his baseball cap as if he was waiting for clearance from the control tower for takeoff. No helmet on this guy. He wasn't

The man called Manfred pedals his way through Ontario. Note he is riding without a helmet and in jeans. Inside his huge green bag is, among other things, 19 pairs of socks. (Photo by Marty Basch).

wearing riding shorts either. He preferred to pedal while wearing jeans. He introduced himself as Manfred from Switzerland, took a watermelon out from a plastic bag on the rear of his load and started to slice it with a knife, giving me a piece as I went to get another bag of ramen noodles.

Manfred had found me after the park attendant told him there was another guy on a bicycle inside.

There are two traits bicycle travelers immediately share — the love of the bicycle and the love of travel. After that, the relationship can range from electricity to static. The initial euphoria of sharing my adventure faded fast, as nary a jolt passed through my body. Manfred could talk. Let's face it, both of us had been on the road for a month. Each had not seen another rider. We were eager for companionship. Within the first hour, during a meal of watermelon and noodles, I learned much about the man called Manfred.

The 27-year-old man had flown to Toronto and began his cross-country ride May 1 from there. Manfred was on his way to Vancouver from where, depending on time, he would either ride his bicycle or take a bus to Los Angles, California. After partying in Los Angeles, he would fly to Costa Rica for a small vacation. His holiday done, a flight would take him then to Colombia where he would be enrolled in a five week Spanish class. Fluent in the language and smart to the culture, Manfred would bicycle down through South America, thus wrapping up his one year adventure. This extravaganza would cost him about $15,000.

Though always fascinating to hear fellow travellers talk about the road, Manfred's broken English soon proved irritating. Listening to the drone became an effort. His speech was peppered with phrases like "have a look" and "it doesn't matter." He called pages in a book "letters." My smile became forced. He told me of his $400 tent and $700 bicycle. In just short of an hour, I longed for solitude again.

We discovered we were taking the same route to Winnipeg, Manitoba. Manfred asked if we could travel together. I heard myself saying "yes." I would have been nearly honest with "we'll see." What I really wanted to say was "no."

The change from riding by yourself to being with a stranger for 24 hours a day isn't easy, especially when you realize it is a mistake. Riding solo, you pick up some habits that just aren't appropriate for when you are with another person.

For example, there is the issue of blowing your nose while riding a bicycle. Cold mornings are the perfect incubators for producing runny noses. Such is spring in Ontario.

It doesn't make much sense to dismount all the time, take out a tissue and honk. There are a few ways to get around this. One way is to keep tissues in the handlebar bag. Long distance riders are adept at zipping open the bag, finding the tissue, blowing, putting the used paper back in the bag and then zipping it closed again all while still pedaling. One could also use the same method with bandanas. Of course, it must be washed before using it as a headband again.

Many riders though prefer to just lean to one side of the bicycle and blow. Right-handed riders tend to lean to the left, cover the right nostril with the left index figure and exhale. Southpaws seem to prefer a lean to the right with the right index finger covering the left nostril. Covering the nostril means more pressure and force is exerted through the uncovered opening, thus removing the unwanted mucous more quickly.

The mucous, if it doesn't catch on the rider's shoulder, then flies through the air behind the cyclist and lands somewhere.

But if there is a rider behind the nose-blowing cyclist, the one in the rear has to dodge the bullet, so to speak.

Manfred was a stronger rider so I rode behind him.

He had a runny noise. He leaned to the right.

He ticked me off.

Manfred liked carrots. He would eat them for breakfast — while riding. His jacket was seemingly bottomless. He would reach in, take out a carrot and chomp. When he was done, he would spit out the end and fire off another bullet.

It ticked me off.

For four days and over 200 miles, I rode behind Manfred. I listened to him yelling out the distances on the road signs. I could see them. I didn't need a broadcast.

I listened for nearly two days how he would say "Oopsala" instead of "Upsala" for the approaching town. We would go into restaurants for breakfast and he would always order second, and usually the same thing I did.

Together, we cycled through some fairly unpopulated areas dotted with lakes and towns like Shabaqua, English River and Ignace. There were not many campgrounds along this stretch so for two of the three nights we were forced to just pitch tents along the road. One was at a roadside rest area. The other was in a clearing behind some woods. Ontarians can pride themselves on their roadside rest areas. Clean with running water, they are havens for two-wheel warriors. They're also free. We saved money that way, and I would at least attest to sleeping better while traveling with another person.

Manfred was a bright man. A rock climber, he had travelled through much of Europe and was seeing the rest of the world. He knew about keeping the lines of communication open between travellers, always talking about the route, what to eat, where to stay, when to stop. Manfred was a keen gin rummy player. We had a running bet going for a dinner in Winnipeg, the winner of the most games getting the meal from the loser. He probably would have won had we continued riding together. But I wasn't able to switch gears fast enough, traveling by myself and then riding with a stranger.

For a month, I had eaten when and what I wanted. Manfred liked bacon and eggs for dinner. I didn't. I liked to mix macaroni and cheese with vegetables. Manfred didn't. He wanted to build fires every night. I didn't feel like helping.

Cyclists are an eclectic breed. We carry our oddities with us, whether it be in a saddlebag or in our personalities. I certainly have mine and should you meet Manfred one day, perhaps he can tell you his side of the story.

Manfred had his peculiarities and carried them in a huge green bag on the back of his bike. In addition to his front and rear saddlebags, Manfred had this monstrosity on the rear of his bike that had to be the size of a television set. As I rode behind him, I often clicked an imaginary remote to do some channel surfing. The problem was, the damn picture never changed.

Manfred didn't like to do laundry. Inside were his clothes. There were four pairs of jeans, 12 underwear, three pairs of shorts, four pullovers and a world-record I'm sure for bicycle touring, 19 pairs of socks.

Manfred hadn't washed his clothes since he began his trip, over a month ago.

It ticked me off.

On the fourth day, it was time to change the channel. I said goodbye to Manfred on the steps of a closed visitor center in Dryden.

"No problem," he said. I couldn't help feel that I had hurt him, that I had somehow damaged his once-in-a-lifetime trip. I wasn't having fun with him. I too was on a once-in-a-lifetime ride. I did feel sorry as a I rode away, but not that night, at a Dryden campground. Showering for the first time in nearly a week, alone again, mixing my macaroni with tuna fish, I felt alive. I relished the silence. And just for old time's sake, I did some laundry.

Clouds and impending rain greeted me as I zipped open the tent. In Manfred's words, "it doesn't matter." That was true. How perspectives change on the road. Just five weeks ago, no way would I ride in the rain. Now, it was just water. The worst that could happen would be to get wet.

Up and over the hills I went, approaching Eagle Lake and Vermillion Bay, a town where restaurants and a store would be. Instead of the clouds following, I was riding into them and soon enough, the rain began, pelting my gear that was wrapped in plastic.

Harder and harder the rain came down. The skies were dark. Cars had headlights on. But then, they always do in Canada. It's the law. Squinting to protect my eyes from the drops, it became clear I shouldn't be out in this weather. Lightning and thunder danced in the sky. Shelter under the trees by the road was dumb. Each rounded corner brought hopes of an overhang somewhere. There was nothing.

Just outside Vermillion Bay some 30 miles into the day, there was a bank of outhouses. Mini-rivers ran outside the bathrooms. Opening the door, I was thankful there wasn't a stink. With rain on the warpath, I was able to fit my bicycle and gear inside. There was just enough room for me to sit on the john and rest, listening to the rain as it bounced off the wood and plastic.

That was my resting place, until slight claustrophobia and boredom got the better of me. Drenched, how much wetter could I become? I didn't have much time to answer as less than a mile down the road was a restaurant, a place much more welcome than the rain.

Hot coffee, warm eggs and English that wasn't broken was welcome. The rains abated. The check paid. The journey continued.

The squish, squish, squish inside my sneakers was making my feet and mind uncomfortable. A turnout up ahead was a spot to change.

Off came the sneakers, the gloves and the socks. I stood there, wringing out my wet clothes when I felt a presence. I looked up. There, cycling past me, was a smiling Manfred. I saluted. Not a word was spoken between the two of us. He went on.

Initially, his passing didn't interest me. I went back to my roadside laundering. Somehow though, some foolish, juvenile feeling took hold of me. Maybe it was ego, but there was no way I was going to let this 19-pairs-of-sock-carrying, jean-wearing, carrot-chomping chump beat me to Winnipeg or even the next town. He was out of sight, so I started chasing him.

Hilly terrain was about to begin. East of Kenora, a sprawling vacationing spot on Lake of the Woods, is where exposed sections of the Canadian Shield can be seen. The Shield is an area of about 2,000,000 square miles of granite, marble, gneiss and other rock that is millions of years old. Pink is the predominant color, and the shapes of the rocks give the area a lunar feeling. There was an above-treeline flavor with tiny shrubs and trees clinging to the rocks.

It's also a heckuva place to hold a road race.

For miles, up and over, there was no Manfred.

I finally saw him at a rest area. It was a place I should have stopped. No, I didn't listen to my legs. The ego ruled.

I wouldn't look back, but I knew Manfred had seen me.

It took a few miles, but he passed me, never saying a word.

Up and over we went, his baseball cap staying on his head between those two giant ears even at speeds of 35 miles per hour.

The rain started again. There was no shoulder. Blind spots were frequent. Here were two jerks, racing in some idiotic test of manhood in a foreign country on a rainy Monday afternoon. The spray of water underneath the tires intensified with speed. Brakes didn't work as well in the rain. Legs pumped, breathing increased. Adrenaline flowed.

Sometime, somewhere, reason started to take hold. It's not a race. It's not a race, I kept repeating. We weren't the only ones on the road. This was logging country. We could hear the logging trucks coming up from behind. This wasn't worth it, I kept telling myself. I passed Manfred. He passed me going down a hill. I sped up in this wet cat and mouse game and passed him as we zoomed down a hill, riding two abreast, a couple of morons set on suicide. The man was strong. In minutes, he caught me again. It's not worth it, not worth it, I said. I caught him again.

A long hill was up ahead. The mental needle in my exhilaration gauge was inching towards empty. He would pass me on that hill. It was time to admit defeat. With a huge sweeping motion of my left arm, I signaled Manfred to pass. He did. I slipped down into granny gear and spun slowly up the hill. Manfred crested the hill and faded away.

He had won.

Under the Tarp

L ife goes by a bit more slowly on a bicycle. At 10 miles per hour, a lot more is seen. The roadside hosts both trash and treasure. Beer bottles and cans have been discarded. Soiled disposable diapers litter the landscape. No doubt, half naked toddlers have been whirling through the land, hellbent on having a good time. They drink, get drunk, take off their clothes and throw them by the side of the road. Either that, or they are being raised by environmentally insensitive pea-brains.

Trash can also be an indicator of how far you are from fast food. The closer to it, the more soft drink containers, french fry cartons and hamburger wrappers there are on the road. The further away from civilization you are, the cleaner the area.

There's also trash in the form of rubber carcasses, tires that have ripped apart after thousands of miles. There are real carcasses like moose, deer, skunks, dogs, cats, rodents and birds. If you don't see them, you certainly smell them. Auto parts line the road. Some garbage is hauled to the dump and doesn't make it. Glass, wire, plastic and paper also call the shoulder home.

There are also treasures. Change seems to fall from moving vehicles from time to time. Screwdrivers are a popular item too. So are hammers and ice picks, plus the occasional wrench. Bungie cords pop out a lot. There are also baseball caps, t-shirts, underwear, pants, shorts, sweatshirts, jackets and always one shoe. There's never a pair. Well, almost never. If there is a pair, they are usually tied together and are hanging from an overhead telephone or electrical wire.

Food is on the road. You know you're not the only cyclist around when you see a trail of banana peels. But edible food is spotted, like candy bars. Unopened beverages are a welcome relief, although they are a bit warm. Once cycling in Utah during April, I found a couple of cans of beer. There was still snow on the ground which made for excellent refrigeration at a campground that night.

But the most unusual find was discovered just minutes after Manfred had vanished into the distance. He had passed a treasure that was seeking shelter from the rain under a bright orange tarp on the shoulder of the TransCanada Highway. Head down while cycling up the hill, the color caught my eye immediately and forced me to stop. Straddling my bike, I looked down and saw two black canvas tennis shoes. They appeared to be attached to legs. Next to them were two bicycle tires.

"Hello," I cried out to the creature beneath the tarp.

Out popped a head of closely cropped salt-and-pepper hair.

"Hello to you," said the bespectacled man.

The man wore dirty white pants and had layers of jackets on. He looked homeless. But he wasn't.

"You're Bert Johnson," I said.

He nodded.

"I've heard about you."

Word travels faster than cyclists on the road. Some 150 miles back at a store, a woman had told me about an older gentleman who was biking by himself. He had passed through there a few days earlier.

"You'll probably catch up with him," she said.

More hero than homeless, Johnson's story proves that cycling isn't just a young man's game, and adventure doesn't die with age. Adventure lives in the hearts and minds of those who refuse to be idle.

Over the course of the next 18 hours, I learned much about this ex-welder, miner and preacher from Blind River, Ontario. An epileptic, he lost his driver's license in 1987 and took up bicycling to get around. His heart was giving him problems, so in 1991 Johnson had bypass surgery. Four months later, he took his first long distance bicycle trip. He rode from Canada to Texas.

Armed with a pension and limited time (his doctor had given him five years to live), Johnson decided to go on the road again. He was giving himself two years to cycle the perimeter of the United States, making a huge loop back to Blind River. Johnson was just a few weeks

Sixty-nine-year-old Bert Johnson of Blind River, Ontario was taking two years to pedal his way around the perimeter of the United States. Here is he outside Kenora, Ontario on the day he and the author met. (Photo by Marty Basch).

into his trip.

"I got nothing else to do, and I can't sit around doing nothing," said the 69-year-old traveling man under the tarp, after inviting me in as the rains came again.

Johnson looked as if he had outfitted his expedition from a junkyard. His bicycle was affixed with wire baskets in the front and a makeshift rack in the back. On the right side of the handlebars, he has fastened a huge car mirror. The baskets, rack and mirror probably weighed more than the bike.

Across the front of his bike is where he kept his thick journal. Each day he wrote at least one page. Prior to departure, he made a list of every town he would be passing through and made out a form so he could record his observations of each place. In this most precious log were maps, photos and newspaper clips about him. After all, 69 year old heart bypass patients on a 10,000 mile bicycling trip is good copy. Once a month he would send an article to his hometown paper chronicling his adventure.

He didn't carry a tent, preferring to tie a cord between two trees and draping a tarp over it. He did carry two spare tires on the rear of the bike and when he rode, he had a light brown knapsack on his back.

Although he had a helmet, he rarely wore it. It wasn't comfortable for him. Conventional riding gloves didn't suit him. Instead, Johnson cut the fingers off a pair of outdoor work gloves and used them. No, there was not a stitch of spandex or lycra to be found on this traveler.

Johnson was also on a mission to raise awareness about heart disease. A metal sign hung from the rear of his rig, encouraging many a honk from drivers. The sign had a phone number for people to call to make a contribution to heart and stroke awareness.

The rain stopped. Johnson started to pack up his gear. He was heading for Winnipeg too and we were taking the same route.

"Do you mind if we ride together?," I asked.

"The only way to go is solo. I like riding by myself. Less hassles. Plus you don't want to wait up for me," he said.

I assured him I didn't mind and that we would only ride into Kenora together, perhaps share a campsite and go our separate ways in the morning. Johnson agreed.

Johnson would roll up his right pant leg before riding so his pant leg wouldn't get caught in the chain. Every few miles or so, he would stop to rest. If there was a hill, he would walk it. This man still averaged about 50 miles a day.

With all the weight he was carrying, Johnson wouldn't stick near the edge of the road. He would weave into the middle of the road, making anyone riding behind him on a bicycle nearly become a bypass customer as well. Every car that passed would get a wave from Bert. After a heavy logging truck would go by, Johnson would say, "How did you like that growler?"

Riding with Johnson was fun. It wasn't too long before we found a site in Kenora and a Greek restaurant in town.

"I see more life on the road than I ever do at home," Johnson confided over dinner.

As Johnson was saying that, I thought about Manfred and how he had passed the bright orange tarp on the road and missed the life that stirred beneath it.

The Prairies and Alberta

Bicycle Touring 101

The seemingly never-ending province has ended. The hills of Ontario, home for nearly 1400 miles, are gone. Instead, it's flat. Had the 1400 miles been ridden in the United States, they would have passed through New York, Ohio, Michigan, Wisconsin and Minnesota.

Hills, when was the last one? No longer are thoughts about what's over the next hill, but what's over the next horizon. Grasslands have replaced trees. The road shimmers with imaginary water in the distance. Towns are seen long before they are entered. Though there are many differences between the provinces, there is a similarity. They both are sites of flat tires.

Just miles into Manitoba, after a woman at the tourist information center assured me there were two more hills, then that's it, the rear wheel lost life. It went flat.

Patching was no problem, but I couldn't resuscitate the victim with the pump. Seems a 39-cent piece was cracked and the vital tool was useless. Finally, the terrain was flat, the wind was at my back, yet the travel gods laughed, and laughed hard. They made me walk five miles to the nearest gas station. But the gods then rewarded me with seeing a black bear by the side of the road.

The sighting, near the ranger office in White Shell Provincial Park, was uneventful. The creature was a blur from the corner of an eye. What an odd dog that was lumbering across the road, I thought. It wasn't until I replayed the events of the day in my mind that I saw the bear.

With the tire patched, I thought everything would be fine. But the next day, it was the computer software that wasn't working. The fax program in the computer wouldn't cooperate. A provincial park employee directed me to the local computer whiz. His name was Mike Vlasman, who also happened to be the principal of the Falcon Beach School. It being a school day and the 46 kids in kindergarten through 8th grades in class, Vlasman talked me into giving the students a lecture about my bike trip after he pointed out the problem in the software. I had typed in a wrong phone number in the wrong place.

Bicycle Touring 101 then began for the fifth through eighth graders. The class was a bit of math (converting kilometers to miles), geography and gym. The kids were inquisitive. They didn't know where Maine was, but the instructor couldn't name all the Canadian provinces either. Questions were flung at me: How many miles a day do you ride, where do you sleep, why do your carry three water bottles, what's the hardest hill, what do you eat, how did you train and can you balance your bike on your head?

The questions were answered: An average of about 50 miles per day; campgrounds; it's necessary; any one that makes you walk; lots of food; told my friends I was going to do this; and I doubt it.

The class was also interested in travel with a computer. In the few weeks I had been on the road, I told them I found that newspapers had been my best friends. They were always receptive to letting me use their phones to transmit my stories. However, it didn't work all the time. Every so often, I couldn't get an outside line with my computer and a back-up plan was developed quickly.

The first time his happened was in Kapuskasing, Ontario. I rode over to the *Northern Times* newspaper, introduced myself, explained my situation and asked for a spot to transmit my stories. They complied. However, I was unable to do so. A receptionist suggested to print out the stories and she would fax them to the three newspapers. I thanked her, but didn't want her to go to the trouble. As it so happened, the rival newspaper, *The Daily Press*, was across the street. I walked over there and the same thing happened. I went back to the *Northern Times*, printed out the story and she faxed them.

My batteries lasted about two hours, so I was always on the lookout for outlets. As campgrounds opened, they were always a place because they had them for RV's. I would look on the outside of buildings as well. While doing laundry, I could often find an outlet too. Libraries were a good spot to plug in. To conserve power, I would often take my computer into a rest room at a campground, plug it into the outlet reserved for electric razors and type my journal there. The kids liked that one and laughed. Apparently they had active imaginations.

The kindergarten through fourth graders were a tougher bunch. Their attention span lasted seconds. Since the "class" was being held outside, the tykes started digging in the dirt as the visitor rambled on. It wasn't until the computer was pulled out that the children paid attention. But it waned when they discovered the only game on the hard drive was "Hangman."

These small people did leave a lasting impression. Their questions were more thought-provoking than the older bunch. One question stayed with me throughout the miles, and it took several days for me to answer.

"Which is your favorite water bottle?," piped one of the children. There were three to chose from — the blue one, the purple one and the red one. At the time, the question was laughed off with, "I like them all." It wasn't until many miles later on, that I realized I really liked my purple one the best. It just had a better feel to it.

I moved on, and with the body and bicycle working as one, made the 95 miles into Winnipeg in one day. The city was easy to get into, and later, out from. Jan flew here. She breathed fresh life into mine. Together we explored the city for a few days. She brought lots of food, but left the baskets behind. She also brought a new rear tire for me as the one I was on looked beat.

Culture was needed and here it was found. Dim sum replaced the noodles and macaroni and cheese of the road in two visits to Chinatown. The streets were alive with the colors of many different people. The bike was left in a hostel and the legs were used to walk along the Red and Assiniboine Rivers to an outdoor meeting place called The Forks, Winnipeg's version of Boston's Fanueil Hall and New York's South Street Seaport.

Osbourne Village was Winnipeg's East Village, waking up as the sun set (at about 10 p.m.) with youth donning shaved heads, multi-pierced ears and backwards baseball caps. The Museum of Man and Nature shared lessons of Arctic, urban and maritime life.

After a few days, Jan left.

The tears flowed down my face as the road soon changed. The

TransCanada goes across Canada to Vancouver, but I won't be on it. Soon, the Yellowhead Highway beckoned for the next leg of my trip. The road is named for an Indian trapper who had a streak of yellow in his hair. The prairie highway goes to Saskatoon, Saskatchewan and into Edmonton, Alberta. From there, another road heads to Dawson Creek, British Columbia and the start of The Alaska Highway.

After about four weeks in one province, it's a pleasure to be traveling through several. As the miles clicked by, Alaska no longer seemed as unreachable as it once did.

Fighting the Invisible Warrior

There is always wind on the prairies. It is relentless.

"When we say there isn't any wind, we don't really mean there isn't any wind. What we really mean is there isn't a lot of wind," said Charlene Mills, a student at the University of Saskatchewan.

Flags ripple as do the yellow fields of canola or green tracts of alfalfa, wheat and barley. The wind can sandblast your face, turning it colors far faster than the sun. The wind can make your ears numb to sound. The constant whine becomes white noise. It pounds grain elevators and wails across the train tracks. You daydream and drift.

You can see it too, making waves in the tall grass, like a powerful advancing army, slaughtering everything.

This is a silent killer, one that can drive you crazy. The wind, the invisible warrior, can be a wall. In your face, pounding, it can wear you down. Triple, quadruple your effort and you still go half the distance.

Oh, it can psychologically render a person a vegetable, making him babble to the prairie dogs in the tall grass or killdeer and hawks flying overhead.

When the wind is the devil, the odometer joins his army. Five, six, maybe seven miles per hour is on the digital readout instead of 12, 13 or

14 on this flattest of terrain. It is hard to see the beauty around you as you curse the strongest of enemies.

But others see you, like Michael Thiele of Minnedosa, Manitoba. His red pick-up truck came to a halt when he saw me sitting, spinning and going no where against 36 mile per hour gusts.

"You need lunch," he said. He was right and Thiele introduced me to a heartland delight — the "smorg," an all-you-can-eat chicken, ribs, potatoes, soup, salad and more extravaganza. After two helpings, the winds hadn't subsided. Thirty miles for the day was good enough and Thiele, a vegetarian in meat and potatoes country, invited me and my satiated stomach to his place.

Thiele worked for a Manitoba conservation group and in the afternoon set out to talk to farmers about how they could be better stewards of the land. He also pointed out mallard nests that the group had made and the day ended with the planting of trees for shelter belts, tree groves designed to ward off wind, snow and sun.

Throughout this, the wind howled down the straight, dusty back roads of Manitoba.

"It'll be better tomorrow," he said.

He was right.

When the wind is at your back, it is like having an invisible fighting army pushing you with little effort. The beauty of the prairies comes to life. Horses and cows follow you along in the early hours of the day. Farmers wave hello. The tall grass weaves and bobs, rooting you on to faster speeds. The digital readout on the odometer is the greatest thing you can see as speeds of 24, 25 and 26 miles per hour are reached on the flattest of terrain.

That was a day I would always remember. I rode from Minnedosa, Manitoba to Churchbridge, Saskatchewan. I crossed into a new province. I entered another time zone. The distance was 118 miles. It was a personal best, smashing a record 108 miles achieved when I was 16.

When the wind is out of the east, it usually brings rain. The sky is so big here that you can see it coming. So you prepare for it. So far, it hasn't lasted that long. The rain can also fall at night. That's the best time for it.

The wind is constant, though usually not as forceful in the early and end of the day. It hits the tent at night, reminding those inside that it is out there, waiting.

The wind likes to play games too. It can't stay in one place too long. Pop into a restaurant for a meal. Come out and see the flags that have since changed direction.

When the wind is from the northwest, cycling days are short, about 40 miles. The odometer is set on the stopwatch mode so it doesn't drive the rider insane with its low readings.

When the wind is from the southeast, cycling days are heaven with 80-mile plus days. The odometer readings are welcome.

On the flats, riders earn every mile. Coasting is minimal. The legs are pistons, forever working. Yes, here on the hot prairies, you work. It is a place to get stronger, both physically and mentally.

Roadside Justice

There isn't much in Borden, Saskatchewan, some 30 miles west of Saskatoon. There's a small park, a spur road and the Kozy Korner restaurant. Oh, there's more. But it's the Kozy Korner along the Yellowhead Highway that is memorable.

It wasn't the pancakes, ham and coffee that made this dining establishment shine. Nor was it the dozen or so stools lining the counter where local farmers sat sipping coffee, eating toast, talking about the rain fall and watching television during the June 22nd morning.

No, it was a thief.

As was the custom, I would lean my bicycle against something when I would go in for a meal. Something at the Kozy Korner turned out to be the restaurant itself. I would fasten the chin strap of my bicycle helmet and hang it from the handlebars. Into the inverted helmet went my riding gloves. I didn't lock anything. What could happen in the middle of nowhere?

I slid into a booth, ordered the breakfast and eavesdropped on the conversations around me while a pair of starstruck lovers were getting married right there on national, or was it international, television.

Soon I was into my own thoughts. The meal vanished into my stomach. I paid the tab, and left.

I went to the bicycle, not really paying attention, and reached for the helmet. I caught air. The helmet wasn't there.

Slight panic set in. There on the ground, next to the bike, was my blue right riding glove. The other was gone.

A tingling sensation started to creep through my body. I looked around for the missing items. They weren't around.

Picking up the lone glove, I went pack into the Kozy Korner.

"Um, excuse me," I said to the assembled. "But somebody ripped off my helmet."

"You're kidding," was the common reaction of the 10 or so people in the restaurant.

"Welcome to Borden," said one sarcastic patron.

They were reassured, and as if they didn't believe what this stranger was saying, a few of them went outside to verify that the helmet they had never seen before was indeed not there.

Well, this was now the talk of Borden and if they had a daily newspaper, no doubt this was front page news. Soon, talk got around to the guy who had peered through the restaurant window maybe 15 minutes before.

"He had long hair," said one.

"He was wearing a leather jacket and baseball cap," said another.

"Yeah, and he was riding a motorcycle," piped in a man who had been sitting by the window.

We now had our suspect. The waitress got on the phone to the police and gave a description of the jerk. While she was doing this, the Kozy Korner owner bought me a cup of coffee.

The waitress hung up and told me to stay put. The police — the Royal Canadian Mounted Police — were on their way and wanted me to wait for them.

Great, I thought, Dudley Do-Right was going to show up in his red uniform on a dark stallion and gallop through the streets of Saskatoon, where the thief was probably heading, in search of my bicycle helmet.

This was ridiculous. My New York upbringing soon kicked in, and I figured this sleazeball was long gone. After about 15 minutes, I thanked the folks for their help and figured I'd just pick up a helmet in the Battleford's, the nearest population center west. It was just a helmet and glove. The police had more important work. This was Canada. They had to arrest poachers. I told the folks there I would be heading west and the cops could flag me down if they needed me. Besides, was the creep dumb enough to be wearing the thing?

It was a strange sensation riding without a helmet and gloves after being accustomed to those necessary touring accoutrements for nearly two months. I had a bad case of hat head and soon wore my baseball cap.

As I pedaled over the miles I was thinking about my next column. How about something like, "The most expensive breakfast I've ever had."

About ten miles passed when an RCMP car pulled in front of me and the officer in front motioned for me to pull over.

Out stepped Constable Dan Small.

"I hear you're missing a helmet," he said. "What brand was it?'"

I told him.

The constable reached in through the window of the front seat and pulled out a helmet.

"This yours?," he asked.

I smiled.

I reached behind my back to the pocket of my riding shirt and pulled out the lone blue glove.

"You wouldn't happen to have the other one of these, would you?," I asked the constable.

The police officer looked into the front seat again, reached in and took out a red duffle bag. As he was doing so, I saw something in the backseat. There was the guy, the guy with the long hair, baseball cap and leather jacket. He didn't look too happy.

He was handcuffed.

When I looked at him, he turned away.

Constable Small put the duffle bag on the trunk of the car. There wasn't much traffic on the Yellowhead, but what there was slowed down to take a look at this most interesting situation.

The duffle bag was zipped open and Constable Small reached in. He took out a sweat shirt. Then came a pair of shorts. Next was a blue riding glove — the smoking glove. He gave it to me.

The constable went back to the car and got out his notepad to take my statement right there by the side of the road. I filled him in on what had happened and what had been taken.

Constable Small had gotten the call from the waitress. He happened to be heading east on the Yellowhead. The creep had decided to travel west, not east as I had imagined.

"How did you find him?," I asked.

"It wasn't too difficult," said Constable Small. "He was the only motorcyclist wearing a bicycle helmet."

"Unbelievable," I said, giving another glance at the backseat while shaking my head.

In Canada, it is mandatory for a motorcyclist to wear a helmet.

Small surmised the suspect didn't have one, so he acquired mine outside the Kozy Korner although he told Small he had found it.

The creep, my word not Small's, also had a criminal record. He had taken part in such leisurely activities as theft, mischief and failure to appear. Plus, the slime had just gotten out of jail just two months before!

Also, it seems Mr. Longhair didn't have any registration papers for the Honda CX-500 he was operating. He didn't have a license either.

Constable Small figured the guy might spend a few months in jail for his efforts.

I thanked him for delivering his swift brand of roadside justice and apologized for not waiting at the Kozy Korner.

"You've got to have faith. It doesn't always end up like this," said the constable before he got back into the car and kicked up some dust as he revved his horsepower into the sunset.

That's true, but for me the Mounties still always get their man.

This whole incident had me in stitches, and it was evident as I continued on the journey with a grin bigger than Detroit. That grin got even bigger as I stopped to take a look at the motorcycle the thief was riding since it was now a fixture by the side of the road. The front light was cracked. I took a few pictures.

Still, this amazing tale was too much for me to contain. After seven weeks on the road, I had done enough talking to myself. I needed an audience.

I figured I would find it in a phone booth.

There in a booth next to a gas station was the local yellow pages. I flipped through it, looking for the community newspaper. However, the

Saskatoon paper had a toll-free number. That made it the winner.

I dialed the number, asked for the newsroom and started to tell my story to the voice on the other end.

The next day, I picked up *The Star Phoenix* and glanced through it. On page two, was an item that started with the headline, "Bicycling U.S. reporter marvels over Mounties. It read:

> A New Hampshire newspaper reporter was impressed with the "marvellous Mounties" of Saskatchewan Wednesday.
>
> Marty Basch, who is pedalling a bicycle to Alaska, stopped for coffee in Borden in the morning.
>
> While he was inside the coffee shop, his helmet and one glove disappeared from the handlebars of his bike.
>
> Police were called.
>
> "About 10 miles further down the road, a police car pulled me over. Const. (Dan) Small asked me what kind of helmet I had. Then he took a helmet out of the car. I asked about the glove. He gave me the glove," said the reporter, who is filing stories to his home state and an Alaskan newspaper during the course of his travels.
>
> He carries a laptop computer with him.
>
> "I was impressed with the roadside justice. Those marvellous Mounties," Basch said.
>
> Police arrested a person in connection with the incident.
>
> The suspect was riding a motorcycle, which Small said had been reported stolen.

Yes, that was true roadside justice.

Friday came and it was time to call Jan. I couldn't wait to tell her about the motorcycle man. Every person I had met since then was forced to sit and listen to the story.

It brought a good laugh to all. There were even a few who could telegraph the story and provide the punchline. They still would get a laugh. But nothing prepared me for the conversation with Jan.

"You're not going to believe this story. I.....,"

"Got your helmet stolen," said Jan.

The phone line went silent.

"How? What the f....? How did you know?," I asked.

"It was on the radio," she said.

A colleague of Jan's had been listening to WMWV that morning in North Conway, New Hampshire, over 2,000 miles and another country away from Borden, Saskatchewan. There was a short item on the news. Jan's friend heard it and went to work. Jan hadn't heard it since she rarely listens to the radio in the morning.

At work, Jan's friend told Jan.

Now Jan told me.

I was flustered, speechless, stupefied.

Two things could have happened: An editor at *The Star Phoenix* had contacted the Associated Press, a wire-service that provides news from newspapers to other newspapers around the world, and given them the story.

The other scenario was that an editor at the Associated Press had seen the story in *The Star Phoenix* and distributed it through the network.

Whichever it was, the story of my bicycle helmet had reached home before I could reach out and touch someone, let alone write my column about.

Also, when I returned from my trip, I learned other friends in different parts of New Hampshire had either heard or read about it.

All of this had happened because some guy hadn't bothered to steal a motorcycle that came with a helmet.

But what happened to the guy?

He went to jail.

Several months after the trip was completed, I contacted Constable Small and asked him about the fate of the man. I learned his name — would you believe Martin?

He was born November 21, 1971. I'll spare his last name in print. He won't be in jail forever.

Martin was charged with two crimes. One was possession of stolen property of a value over $1,000. That was for the motorcycle. The other was possession of stolen property of a value not over $1,000. That was for the helmet.

Trial was set for November 17, 1994 in Saskatoon. Originally, Martin pleaded not guilty to the charges. He changed those pleas just before the trial started.

For stealing the motorcycle, he was sentenced to two months in jail, ordered to pay $450 in restitution to the motorcycle's owner for damage he caused and was placed on probation for 15 months. For snatching my helmet, he received a sentence of 30 days to be served concurrently with the first.

That's roadside justice.

Rain On Me

"Wet enough for you," said the stranger.

I just smiled, but inside I wanted to pop the sucker.

Yes, it has been wet enough for me. It has rained every day for seven straight days. There has been drizzle and downpours, pea-sized hail and miserable black clouds.

Sometimes the rain comes in the morning. Other times it doesn't start until evening and pelts the tent all night in a water torture exercise that will keep me up all night.

And then, it can rain all day.

Faced with a day spent in a tiny tent or riding in the rain with steady 18 wheeler-generated tsunamis drenching me, I'll take the wet. While on a bike trip, the idea is to keep moving. As for staying dry, forget it.

The sneakers get soaked, squish when you walk and become so rank they will keep any bear away. Socks turn black with mud. Legs became crusted with grit. Riding gloves get wrung out regularly.

Everything gets wrapped in plastic bags — sometimes twice. The computer, entombed in a soft case and dry bag, escapes the wetness.

Any overhang becomes a haven. More coffee is drunk at meals to keep me inside and dry.

At least there aren't any bugs. Yet.

The rain too has brought with it some bad luck. Now at the 3,000 mile stage, it is inevitable that parts will wear and need replacement. In Lloydminster, a town that straddles the provinces of Alberta and

Saskatchewan and has a long yellow line running down a street to prove it, a bike mechanic named Garth Sired at the High Gear Cycle and Sports shop on 49th Street discovered a broken tooth on my second chain ring.

He didn't have a quality replacement part. Instead, he filed down the broken tooth as best he could and tuned up my bike to get me to Edmonton. He didn't charge me for the service.

"Right on," as they say in Canada.

I made the 150 miles to Edmonton and found a shop that had quality replacement parts. The ring, chain and freewheel were all replaced.

"You shouldn't have any problems," were the famous last words of the bike tech.

The next day it started to rain, and the problems started.

Every day my chain would fall off. Every day I would put it back on. Four days after it was put on, the chain broke. A link had snapped. This happened about a mile out of Fox Creek, Alberta on Canada Day, the nation's independence day. Only food and gas stores were open. There is no bike shop. Not being a handy sort of guy, I opted to stay in town, wait until the hardware shop opened in the morning and watch the rubber duck races, jaws of life demonstration by the fire department and partake of the barbecue.

The next day, an employee of the hardware store who happened to be a single mom with long finger nails ("When you're a single mom you learn to do everything," she said) and a customer worked outside the store to replace the link.

You'd figure someone cycling from Maine to Alaska would know how to do this stuff. Not me. I can fix a flat. That's about it. But I carry the tools figuring I'll find someone who can help me. It's a bad philosophy, I know. Self-sufficiency is key on the road. So far I've been lucky.

With the chain fixed, I continued. The bike was shifting itself and something was making a grinding sound. I was not happy.

Grande Prairie is about 300 miles northwest of Edmonton, near British Columbia. It is a city of some 30,000 and is the last major population center I will hit until Whitehorse, Yukon over 800 miles away. The city is about 80 miles from the beginning of The Alaska Highway. The work had to be done there.

The gears were badly out of tune. They were adjusted.

The grinding sound came from dirt sneaking into the rear hub. It was cleaned and repacked. The rear brakes had worn down. They were replaced.

So the mechanic finished his work and told me to take the bike for a spin. I headed through the back alley, made a right, stopped at a red light, made another right, pedaled a few seconds and heard a loud Sssssssssss. My rear tire was flat.

It can only get better. Right?

The Alaska Highway

The Road That Fear Built

The idea of bicycling a road that slices through wilderness excited me. The Alaska Highway is the land link, the "Yellow Brick Road," that connects Alaska to the rest of the world. The two-lane road would wind through muskeg, mountains, mosquitoes and mud for 1,422 miles from Dawson Creek, B.C. to Delta Junction, Alaska and then to Fairbanks for a total of 1,520 miles. Two countries would make contact. Another time zone would be entered. The people who travel and live along it would have stories to tell.

Finally, after cycling over 3,400 miles, through four states, four provinces and having four flats, the trip for me had finally begun on July 6 in Dawson Creek. It is here the highway begins. Highway isn't a good word to really describe it. The Alaska Highway is more of a country road. It isn't an eight-lane super expressway. It's more a two-lane ride through the bush and a few natural treasures. Speed isn't the essence; travel is.

Dawson Creek is up there. Three thousand miles from New York, some 3,800 miles from Miami, Dawson Creek is home to 12,000 people. Perceived from the confines of a city, it is in the sticks. From the saddle of a bicycle, it a place that has everything a cyclist needs before setting out on the highway.

History is king in Dawson Creek. Right there underneath the maroon grain elevator bin is the beginning of the highway. There's a sign that evens says so. "You are now entering World Famous Alaska Highway," it declares. There's a monument with a few plaques on it. Travelers take turns taking pictures by the thing.

They then head into the museum and learn about the road they are about to take. The Alaska Highway was built during a time of fear. World

War II was being fought and the Japanese had bombed Pearl Harbor in Hawaii. Alaska, many thought, was the next step for the invasion. An overland road was needed to connect the Lower 48 to Alaska so military transports could get through. The idea was rammed down the throats of the Canadian government. The highway was already under construction when the Canadians put their signature to paper. Ten thousand troops and 6,000 civilians began construction on March 9, 1942 and completed it in just eight months and 13 days.

Not much is left of that original road. The grades were steep. The stretches often narrow, muddy and impassable. One section of the road was called Suicide Hill. The grade so extreme, there was a warning sign posted 200 feet from the hill during the early years of the highway. "Prepare to meet thy God," it said.

The highway now gets an annual facelift. The grades are, for the most part, moderate to accommodate modern travelers in recreational vehicles and huge trucks that transport goods to the north. Construction wasn't easy. Over fifty years ago, the land the highway would pass through was wilderness. Indigenous people called it home. Workers toiled seven days a week. In the winter, sub-zero temperatures froze both men and machine. Supplies were scarce. In spring, mud proved another stifling hurdle, slowing progress to a crawl. Summer came, and with it, mosquitoes and black flies which feasted on the fresh blood carried in the bodies of men. There were accidents and deaths.

Construction began concurrently at two ends. One camp worked out of Fort St. John, near Dawson Creek. The other was based in Whitehorse, in the Yukon. The road followed existing roads, rivers and Indian trails. One day, the two camps met in the Yukon at a place called Contact Creek.

The road was complete. Throughout the road would be signs detailing the history , the road and the people who had once lived there. Mileposts are set up to click off distances. It would be a bit confusing. Some are in kilometers, as Canada uses the metric system. Others are in miles. Some are in historical miles, using the original road as the measurement. Others are in today's miles. However, the road is well-marked in terms of distance.

There is the official Mile 0 of the highway located in the center of Dawson Creek at the center of 10th Street and 102 Avenue. It is a white sign post with three flags perched on the top. On it are distances from

Dawson Creek to Fort St. John (48 miles), Fort Nelson (300 miles), Whitehorse (918 miles) and Fairbanks (1,523 miles). The post isn't on a corner or anything. It's smack in the center of a junction. It was fun watching the tourists dodge the traffic to get to it for that all-important photo.

I arrived in Dawson Creek mid-morning that July Wednesday, cycling from a roadside camping area in Alberta. A new province, a new challenge waited. Time was spent stuffing my face with fresh apple crisps and stocking up on cans of beans, ramen noodles, peanut butter and more. I picked up some mail that had been delivered to me via general delivery and just walked around the town. I also stopped into a bank and cashed in a few hundred dollars worth of traveler's checks. From the appearance of things, it didn't look like there were going to be too many ATM machines, let alone banks, along the Alaska Highway.

The first night on the road was spent along Mile 17. There is a campground there called the Alaska Highway Campground and RV Park. That was home for the night after only 17 miles on the highway.

The appeal of staying there was found in what waited just a few hundred yards down the road — the curved Kiskatinaw River bridge. This 531-foot span crossed the brackish, brown, muddy waters of the Kiskatinaw. The bridge was also the only remaining original timber bridge left on the highway. The campground, and the bridge was on a rare section of road, the old Alaska Highway. The campground was just a slight detour down some very hilly terrain off the main road. I had to cycle the old road.

Aside from the history, that night at the campground provided a glimpse into nights to come. Each day around 4 p.m., travelers would begin to pull into a campground. They were either coming from or going to Alaska. Alaskans were escaping their state and the influx of tourists. The tourists were heading to Alaska to feed the coffers of those left behind. They would share tales, meals and drinks. Many were retirees. Others were adventurers on their own trips in VW buses filled with stickers and Grateful Dead tapes . While I was going along at 50 miles per day, they were moving on at 50 miles per hour. They would click off places I had been a week ago and they had only been there that morning. They were talking of places to get to tomorrow night that I might pedal to in 10 days. Veteran highway riders told of previous trips. Rookies told of hopes. Some vehicles rattled in. Others had cracked windshields. Inside each one was a tale adding to the reputation of this northern, wild road.

But what every conversation seemed to entail was the condition of the road. If there is a bible for the highway rider, it is called "The Milepost." It seems no RV is without one. The 46th edition of this guidebook was being sold virtually everywhere, at every campground, motel, gas station and restaurant. Updated annually, the book breaks down each highway in Alaska, northern Alberta, British Columbia, the Northwest Territories and the Yukon mile by mile. Every location of a trash barrel, roadside turnout and accommodation is in there. It will tell you how far it is from here to there, where to look for wildlife and where to call for help.

Because of its size, is in impractical for a cyclist to carry. But the savvy cyclist can save the cost of the book and borrow one for a few minutes every night. On the Alaska Highway, as what was made clear to me that night, was if you have a question, ask someone in an RV. They will then go inside their rig, produce the book and let you read it. It has the answer to virtually everything.

Road conditions were a concern because they were constantly changing. Summer was a time for nipping and tucking the highway. The guide is frank about conditions. They range from poor to excellent. Poor might be chuckholes, gravel breaks, deteriorating shoulders, frost heaves and bumps. Road crews would be out patching the holes. They would be digging up the road. Actually, there would be no road as you would expect. It would be dirt.

If the road was particularly poor, construction crews would stop traffic and then have a pilot car, or guide, lead the procession through the gnarly terrain.

Briefly, the guide summed up what the road would be like. Good pavement existed for the first 300 miles. Then, as the road crossed the Rocky Mountains, watch for narrow and winding roads with a few rough spots. Between the British Columbia and Yukon borders to Haines Junction in the Yukon, the road ranges from fair to excellent. Between Kluane National Park in the Yukon and Beaver Creek, the most western town in Canada, look for some rough road. The highway between Beaver Creek and the United States border was apparently in very rough shape. Then it's back to excellent.

Also at this point, I was meeting people from communities I had cycled through. They always wanted to know what places of interest I had seen. They also made it clear there would be times a guy on a bicycle would be cursing the road.

Even RV's Get the Blues

Rain provides many excuses for the traveler. It's an excuse not to ride. It's an excuse to read a book or write in a journal. On day three of the highway, it was an excuse to do laundry in Pink Mountain, at Mile 143. Pink Mountain is typical of the many small towns along the road. The population is under 100. There's a place to camp, a motel, a post office, a gas station and a laundry. Sometimes these things are all under the same roof.

Pink Mountain was bigger in the sense that it had two motels and one campsite. It was at the campsite I was doing laundry and therein, met Chuck and Collette Graham.

Baseball caps, t-shirts and sweatshirts are now souvenirs people can't do without when they visit somewhere, and on that Friday in British Columbia, Collette was wearing one emblazoned with "Cape Cod." Cape Cod is in New England and New England is my home. This was a natural conversation opener to chat with Collette, doing laundry with another woman.

The Grahams were traveling from Billerica, Massachusetts to Alaska in their RV. Retired, they now take to the road as often as possible, crisscrossing the nation and were on their first trip to Alaska.

Collette introduced me to her husband Chuck and extended an invitation to join them for dinner in their RV.

I said yes.

Going from a tent with the pitter-patter of rain echoing through the narrow confines into a long, carpeted and furnished recreational vehicle is like being transported from the desert to the shores of a clear, unpolluted lake. I felt underdressed. Was there a dress code? On these wheels was a bedroom , kitchen and dining room. They was a television, books, magazines and newspapers. There was even a refrigerator. My goodness. So much food could be stored in these things! That's cold milk. No more evaporated stuff for me!

We talked about travel and family. They talked about their farm back in Billerica and how every Christmas Chuck pulls the grandchildren around on a tractor. The Grahams had 18 grandchildren. They talked about children and how they kept in touch with them.

I spoke about my trip. They were curious, having only seen bicycling tourists from way up high in the driver's and passenger's seats at the front of the moving home. My visit lasted several hours over dinner and the Grahams extended another invitation, to join them and their family for Christmas in Billerica. Although I did not make it to Massachusetts that Christmas, I did stay in touch with the Grahams. What happened to them just days after that glorious lasagna dinner needs to be added to the tales of people traveling the Alaska Highway.

The Grahams continued their northward quest in their 33-foot long Holiday Rambler. This was the fifth year they were using it and it had never given them any trouble. On July 9, they were about 54 miles from Fort Nelson, when they heard a slapping noise coming from one of the two engines. Chuck first thought it was the fan belt. But it was worse. The engine had blown.

The RV was then towed to Fort Nelson and made its way to Charlie's Truck Repair. The new parts had to be shipped from Canadian company headquarters in Woodstock, Ontario. The right parts initially weren't shipped. There were a few other problems, but the engine was finally repaired — three weeks later. Chuck and Collette were then presented with a bill. It was for $17,000 Canadian.

Undaunted, the Grahams pressed on. They were anxious to see Alaska. They started her up. Chuck got back on the Alaska Highway. What an experience they had back there in Fort Nelson. That surewould be a good story to tell everyone back home.

Six miles later, the Grahams were being towed back to Fort Nelson. The second engine blew.

Back to Charlie's they went. Charlie felt sorry for the Grahams. He insisted they take his new truck and camper to see Alaska.

"You've come this far, you've got to go," he told the Grahams.

The Grahams took off with Charlie's gear. They returned five weeks later.

"The thing wasn't ready. They were having a hard time getting parts," said Chuck, recounting the story a few months after my trip had ended.

It was now September 4. Charlie told the Grahams he thought everything would fixed by Thanksgiving. Thanksgiving Day is different in the two countries. The Canadians were celebrating theirs on October 10th. Still, the Grahams were now getting concerned that they might not get back home until Thanksgiving Day in the United States which was November 24th.

At this point, the Grahams were starting to miss their family. Chuck also had a part-time job for the football season. That was a commitment. They decided to head home.

"It had been a long trip. It makes you more melancholy the longer you're away from the kids. And also, I couldn't' see us freezing up there for another month and a half," he said.

Charlie had a plan. He volunteered to drive the RV to Edmonton during the winter after the work was finished. Chuck would fly to Edmonton, meet Charlie and drive back to Massachusetts. Chuck was reluctant to do so as he was unfamiliar with the frozen roads in the North during winter.

So they came upon another idea. Charlie said he might drive the RV straight to the Grahams house in Billerica at the end of March.

That sounded fine. The Grahams then had to get home.

"Everyone knew us by the time we left Fort Nelson. We even went to church and the priest said, 'I can't believe the two of you are still here.' I'll tell you," said Chuck, "they are a great bunch of people up there. The generosity of Fort Nelson impressed me. They're unselfish, willing to help everyone."

The Grahams did some calling and discovered that it would cost each of them $2,500 to fly home from Fort Nelson. The next option was the train. That way home was $800 apiece, including a 30 hour stopover. They nixed that.

Chuck and Collette ended up taking the bus and getting a senior citizens discount for about $180 each. They left Fort Nelson on a Wednesday and got to Toronto that Saturday. It was a tiring, uncomfortable journey, during which time Chuck's leg started to swell. This concerned Collette and they ended up at a hospital. Chuck didn't get home until after leaving the hospital. That was 13 days later.

"The doctor told me I was going to die, that I had an infection to the heart."

That infection was cellulitis. It is a bacterial infection. Chuck thought he was going to lose his leg. He thought he would die.

He did not.

"It was an experience. If I wasn't with the right partner, this could have been a disaster. I've told a lot of people and they don't know how we did it. You have to just let things roll off your back. You can't get upset," said Chuck.

So while the Grahams spent their winter back in Massachusetts, the RV spent the winter in Fort Nelson.

Chuck also said he and Collette were expecting grandchild number 19 in May, a few months later.

I often wondered which made it to the Grahams first — the child or the RV?

The Trolls of Buckinghorse River

Deep in the land of muddied footwear there lived for a day four trolls on the bridge at Buckinghorse River.

The quartet had left June 7 from Montana and were heading to Skagway, Alaska in search of the mighty dollar.

But all was not well with the four men. They were out of food and broke. So the biking trolls decided on desperate measures.

Here in the hills that spring up from the muskeg, where lightening and thunder scare even the bravest of souls, empty pop (as they say in Canada) and beer cans command five cents each. The four were collecting them in trash bags, putting them on the back of their bicycles and trading them in for cash. However, redemption centers are far between in this lonely, rugged area, and the four needed showers, food and rest quickly.

So they were hitching on the bridge over the fast-moving waters of the Buckinghorse River, 175 miles from where the Alaska Highway began.

Who would pick up four grungy, foul-smelling, unshaven, bicycle-riding fellows on a desolate stretch of road as the rain poured down to make matters worse?

No one.

"What's that?," I wondered as I crested yet another hill and looked down at the bridge.

"What's that?," wondered the trolls as they looked up at the crest of yet another hill. It wasn't a truck, nor a car, nor an RV, nor even a motor-cycle.

When I rode down to the bridge, I was delighted to see the four. The four were delighted to see another rider. That is how I met the four.

There was Frank, about 45, bearded and bespectacled. He was the wise one. Frank was divorced, had driven a cab and had now lived for five years on his bicycle, touring all over North America.

Gary was the red-haired one. Age 24, he had grown up in upstate New York, recently graduated college with a degree in marketing and was now on his first bicycling trip. He hadn't used his degree yet.

Matt was the hungry one. From Atlanta, Georgia, he was in his early 20's. So hungry he was, that in a restaurant called the Buckinghorse River Lodge he asked the waitress for the leftover fries some customers had not eaten. Matt was like a vacuum. The fries were soon gone. Like the others, Matt hadn't showered for days. His hair would stand easily in a mohawk style and he would sing Billy Idol's "White Wedding" while waiting for potential rides. He has one hoop earring in each ear.

Finally, there was Doug, age 21. Also from Atlanta, he was the the-atrical one. Trying to get rides, he would perform mime in the road. Doug would sink to his knees, clasp his hands together and beg. He has a goatee-like beard.

The four had worked together in West Yellowstone, Montana.

I was in search of companionship after several miles of babbling to myself and asked the trolls if I might stay with them for a while.

"Yes," they answered.

So, as honorary troll for a day, I traded stories with my newfound comrades. When the rains came, we would go across the road to the only restaurant for 50 miles and drink coffee. We would then go out again. Sometimes when there weren't any cars, we would go out in the middle of the road and play hackey sack. This wasn't safe, but we did it anyway. Our mothers were thousands of miles away and no one would tell them.

Tired of coffee after a while, the four retired to under the bridge. Matt would stay up top, trying to get a ride.

Underneath, we would play cards. We would watch the swallows dive into their mud castles built on the framework of the bridge. We would watch the bridge flex when a large truck passed overhead. The trucks made a big noise.

When things go wrong, collect cans. That was the philosophy of "The Trolls of Buckinghorse River." That's Frank (l), Matt, Doug (with sign) and Gary. (Photo by Marty Basch).

Soon, we made a fire to stay warm. But the smoke disturbed the birds. So we, the trolls, extinguished the flames and put on more clothes.

We got out our portable stoves and pooled resources for sustenance.

When night fell, we were wet and tired. Doug, Matt, Frank and Gary had tried since the night before to get a ride. They had no luck. This day they had no luck either.

Frank went to sleep under the bridge. Gary and I set up our tents on a grassy section by the restaurant for free. Matt and Doug still tried to hitch.

The next morning was still dark and cloudy. Gary (who later confided he did have some money) and I had breakfast. We did not see the other trolls and figured they had gotten a ride.

We decided to pedal the 125 miles to Fort Nelson together. That was where the other trolls were heading because some weeks before they had sent food and money to a mail stop.

Frank then entered. He said he was going to back to Montana. He had only 27 Canadian dollars left. He would collect cans to get back. He did not know where Doug and Matt were.

Gary gave Frank his bag of cans. I gave Frank two bags of noodles.

Frank thanked us.

Gary and I rode on. We got to Fort Nelson the next day. At the mail stop was a note from Doug and Matt telling Gary and I where they were. Gary and I went there.

There were smiles and stories at the troll reunion. This is the tale Doug and Matt related: They had spent the night across the way from the restaurant in an abandoned motel. When they awoke, everyone else was gone. They went back to hitching.

A van had stopped for them and given them food, but no ride. They were not happy. So they feigned a mechanical problem with Matt taking off his front wheel.

This worked. An RV with four women stopped. Doug said there were problems with the hubs and it could be fixed at a gas station in Fort Nelson. The ladies did not know what hubs were. So Matt, Doug, their bicycles and cans got a ride with four ladies and two Chihuahuas in an RV.

"Imagine that, two more cyclists," said one of the ladies in the RV as it passed a pair of bikers on the way to Fort Nelson.

"Yes, imagine that," said Doug.

Doug and Matt were sad to learn that Frank had gone back to Montana. But the group was still four since I had now become the fourth and the four will now see what is down the Alaska Highway.

A Meal on Wheels Rolls Through Bear Country

The driver of the camper slowed down as he rounded the steep curve and rolled down the window.

"Hey, just thought you would want to know. We saw a bear, a black bear, about 50 yards up," he said.

"Thanks," I said meekly.

They happened to be coming from the direction I was heading which meant the bear was there, waiting.

There wasn't much else to do but push forward. Rounding the bend, I heard a crashing sound and then looked toward the bush. There I saw the rear end of a bear as the beast went back into the woods. That was the fourth bear I had seen since starting the Alaska Highway July 6.

Make no mistake. British Columbia and the Yukon are bear country. Hiding in the trees, stalking rest areas and waiting for the next camper with a cooler are black bears. Everyone along this mostly paved, pot-hole-ridden, gravel-flying, muddy, dust-plagued road through the wild north seems to have a bear story. If it isn't their own, it's borrowed, embellished and passed on.

Bears and tourists meet. Radio newscasts report encounters sporadically. Newspaper articles about roadside meetings are posted in rest areas. Provincial campsites post warnings on bulletin boards. Travel guides forewarn visitors. Bears are the subject of conversations at every gas station, hotel, store and campground. Bears do maul people.

And now here I was riding through bear country.

I felt like a meal on wheels.

Actually, that was the punchline to one of the jokes a local told me. The joke was: What does a bear call a cyclist? The answer: Meal on wheels. Another joke went like this: What does a bear call a cyclist in a sleeping bag? A sandwich.

Amusing? Perhaps the first time. But it probably wasn't all that funny to a cyclist I met along the way named Sherry Higgins. She was on a solo bicycle trip from Alaska to California.

Higgins had been camping in a site by the Tetsa River in British Columbia along the Alaska Highway. Sleeping, Higgins said she "awoke to the nightmare we all hope never happens."

The midnight sun cast a shadow in the form of a bear as a rustling outside her tent awakened Higgins. A black bear was by her bicycle and the feisty rider wasn't about to let the creature rummage and chew through her equipment.

Higgins carried mace with her. She kept it inside the tent at night. The woman got the spray, unzipped the tent and was able to blast two shots of hot pepper into the bear's face. The bear bolted off into the night. Higgins' gear wasn't damaged.

Along the hilly highway, it seems most incidents involve tourists just being stupid. They do the one thing no one should do. They feed the bears. The bears then associate food with people. People drive by in vehicles. They roll down the window. Mom feeds the bear while dad gets out the video camera. Look at mom smiling. Isn't the bear cute? It's so cuddly.

These cuddly creatures then get bolder. They get closer to the cars. If a window doesn't roll down, bears have been known to do it themselves. Except they don't use the handle. They crash through with a massive paw. People get hurt; bears get killed. That's because a bear that links humans to food is a threat to people. Game officers must find the bear and shoot it.

Not all bear attacks are limited to the Alaska Highway. They happen all over. One person I met on the highway was Thane Humphrey of Wasilla, Alaska. He's a family man and the family was on an early July vacation at Lake Laberge in the Yukon, north of Whitehorse along the Klondike Highway.

The Humphreys were staying at a camp when around 9 a.m. one morning he and his eight-year-old daughter heard some shouting outside their cabin. The pair went outside to investigate. They rounded a corner, stopped and came face-to-face with a bear.

"I had her, my daughter, by the hand, and the bear pops out and looks like it wanted us," he said.

The bear did not get what it apparently wanted. Thane and his daughter dashed into the cookhouse and shut the door behind them. The owner of the camp rushed out with a shotgun and blasted the bear dead.

It must be nice to be able to seek shelter in a structure while being chased by a bear. That is hardly the case on a bicycle. Families traveling in their homes on wheels have the luxury of just rolling up the windows. The driver just puts a little more pressure on the accelerator and off they all go, dust and all. There can be a ton or more of metal separating them from the bear. On a bicycle, you are exposed to all elements — weather, insects, crazy drivers and bears. There are no windows to roll up. Many locals were asked for advice on what to do if a biker meets a bear.

"Pedal fast," was the most common response.

Pedaling fast was on my mind as I glanced through the Fort Nelson News one day. In one issue, four bear encounters were reported under the ominous headline, "Higher Number of Bear Human Confrontations Reported on Alaska Highway." Four consecutive days, June 25 to 28, saw four reported encounters on the stretch of road from Fort Nelson to Liard River Hot Springs. That was the road I was about to embark on. Three of the bears were black bears, one was a grizzly. The grizzly was killed as it charged a family. Two of the black bears mauled tourists. Of course, that was after the visitors threw food to the bear. The other bear was acting aggressively, displayed no fear of humans and was eventually shot and killed.

Knowing that bears are in the area forces riders to take precautions. Staying in paid campsites is generally a good idea. Just camping by the side of the road may put you more at risk. Food isn't kept in the tent. Instead, it is hung from a tree. Singing or making loud noises will also keep the bears away.

But that didn't help one cyclist — Giorgio Mazza of Lecco, Italy. The Mazza story is one of the more incredible and famous bear stories kicking around the Fort Nelson, British Columbia area. The tale was told to me by Judith Kenyon, editor of *The Fort Nelson News*. Kenyon was kind enough to let me transmit my columns from the newspaper's offices during my stay in that town. While the columns were zapped, we swapped stories.

The 39-year-old Mazza was bicycling around the world. He had already gone some 14,000 miles before he left the Toad River Lodge on a bright and sunny May 27, 1978 morning. Mazza was enjoying the spring and sang to the new day. About two miles east of the lodge, a black bear attacked the marathon rider without warning.

Mazza saw the bear and dismounted from his bicycle. He talked and sang to the 200-pound beast in hopes it would go away.

It didn't. Instead, the bear stared right into Mazza's eyes, reared and slugged him with a paw, stunning him. The bear eventually sank his teeth into Mazza's skull and dragged him off the road.

"He told me he could hear the bear chewing him," said Kenyon.

The bear had also gnawed on Mazza's arm. The rider was losing blood quickly and began to feel faint. He prayed, thinking he was going to die.

Then a Dawson Creek gold prospector happened to be passing by in his pick-up truck. By then, a camper had also pulled over and the prospector wanted to see what was going on. Mazza's bicycle and packs were still by the highway.

First getting a rifle from his truck, the prospector followed the bear's trail about 100 feet off the road. He saw the bear with jaws clamped on Mazza's arm, still dragging him away.

Now 20 feet from the bear and Mazza, the prospector took aim and fired one bullet, killing the bear.

Mazza survived the ordeal. Kenyon's husband, a surgeon, operated on Mazza for six hours and sewed him up with 200 stitches. When Kenyon published an interview with Mazza 10 days after the attack, she received telephone calls from media all over the world, including the *National Enquirer*.

It truly is an amazing tale, one I hope never to top.

Traveling with Trolls

We waited. It was Tuesday, July 12th and all four of us, Gary, Matt, Doug and I, had agreed to meet at 1 p.m. at the visitor reception center on the west end of Fort Nelson. From there, the four of us would continue down the road together.

Four can travel more cheaply than one. The four of us got along well, and the companionship would be welcome. In the Yukon, where the road forks, the three would head south down the Klondike Highway to Skagway, where they would get jobs, money and then head back to Montana.

I left the newspaper and rode over to the center. Soon thereafter, Gary showed up. He said Matt and Doug would be there shortly.

Then I told Gary about the interview I had done at the Fort Nelson News. Just as I was about to pedal off, Kenyon came out of the offices and called me over.

"Here," she said, sticking out her hand.

"What's this?," I asked.

"Take your friends out to dinner," she said as bills were pressed into my hand.

Not only had Kenyon and I swapped bear stories, but I told her about the trolls I had met as well. Their hard luck story had entered her heart. She gave me $50 Canadian. The boys would be happy.

So Gary and I waited for Matt and Doug.

We looked at the brochures. I plugged my computer into the outlet to recharge it. We drank coffee.

Fifteen minutes went by.

I made a few long distance phone calls to let some people know I was still alive. Gary made a few too.

Thirty minutes went by.

An hour passed.

"Looks like it's you and me," I said.

"I can't believe those guys," Gary said. "Maybe they went out to collect more cans or something and forgot about the time."

That was possible, but highly unlikely. We decided we shouldn't ride out without them. Hanging out at the visitor center wasn't much fun so Gary suggested we stay at the campground across the road and leave Doug and Matt a note.

We did that.

We spent the night at the Westend RV campground. We showered. Gary did go to try and find the two later on. He never found them. While he was gone, I met a couple who were in the process of moving from Manitoba to Whitehorse, Yukon. They invited me to their site for a steak dinner. They ended up giving me the guy's work number in Whitehorse and told me to look them up.

Gary returned. He didn't have steak. He's a vegetarian. He came back without Doug or Matt. Gary was upset.

I tried to cheer to him.

After all, we were $50 richer.

Not the highest point on the Alaska Highway, Steamboat Mountain is the toughest challenge a cyclist will face on the road. The climb is steep and narrow. The cyclist is too busy looking down to the see the views of the Rocky Mountains and Muskwa River Valley. That is, unless he has stopped or is walking his way up.

The 10 percent grade begins about 30 miles north of Fort Nelson and continues up for about 17 miles. It does not matter that a cyclist has pedaled from Portland, Maine or West Yellowstone, Montana to crest this mountain. The mountain is not impressed. It is there to test you, humiliate you and if you make it to the other side, reward you with a downhill.

Even this far north, July is a hot time. Temperatures reach into the 80's and the sun beats down upon you. The black flies, mosquitoes, grasshoppers, gnats and bees are out and about, looking for things to eat. They are usually quite happy when bicyclists pass through, particularly if the riding is uphill. The elements were not in our favor that day. It was hot, steep and the bugs were out.

Each night the author (l) would record the day's events in his laptop computer. Gary (r) also kept a diary, but made entries the old-fashioned way. Here they are by the side of the road on the Alaska Highway. (Photo by Doug Fejes).

Bugs are incredible little creatures. Open your mouth and they fly right in. Sometimes you'll be riding along and hear a splat. That is the sound of a bug crashing into your riding helmet. The helmet serves the same function as the windshield of a car. The bugs also collect in the hairs of your arms and legs. At night, there can be a thin black layering of bugs over the skin.

But as you ascend a steep grade, bugs are at their best. They know you are concentrating on the climb, that every morsel of energy is being transferred into the legs. They know your upper body is helpless. So they swarm around you and eat you up.

First there is one. This insect is the lookout. He sees you and just buzzes around. You don't give him much thought. Then he calls a few more over. They dance around and psych you out. Then the whole neighborhood comes over, infiltrates your nose, mouth and eyes and has a good ol' down-home chow down. The only think missing is music.

You try swatting them, but it does no good after a while. You douse your bandana in bug dope and hang it around you neck, but it doesn't always work. You ascend the mountain, a cyclist walking with a black cloud around him.

It was just one of those days.

There was a respite though. Eleven miles into the climb is the Steamboat Cafe. This lodge is the only thing in Steamboat. To give you an idea of how remote this place was, it didn't have water piped to it. Water was trucked in with huge containers from Fort Nelson. Inside was a place to rest our rubbery legs. Gary would order a grilled cheese sandwich with any available vegetable tossed in like mushrooms or tomatoes. I stuck to a burger and fries.

As we returned to normal, we struck up a conversation with the waitress.

"Did you happen to see a couple of other bikers pass through?," Gary asked.

"Two came through yesterday and I think they were talking about spending the night somewhere along the road," she said.

"One was blonde, the other had dark hair," Gary said.

"That was them," she said.

At least we knew they had been alive 24 hours before.

The next few days Gary and I cycled through some of the more magnificent scenery along the highway — Summit Mountain and Muncho Lake Provincial Parks. We also found we had a good rhythm riding together. Often we would go at our own pace and meet up at a pre-selected spot. We would take turns leading. There was a tolerance between us, an understanding. We were good road companions.

We introduced each other to different types of foods. Gary, Doug and Matt had done a very smart thing before they left on their trip — they sent food packages ahead. Before they left, they contacted some of the lodges along the way and asked if they could send themselves parcels. The lodges complied. The further north we went, the higher prices were becoming. The $10 hamburger did not exist, but at a few establishments that price rang in at just a few cents under. Although the trio was short on cash, at least they had already paid for their food. All they had to do was get to it.

In the packages were wonderful items. It is easy to get into a food rut on the road. Gary unraveled that. After each food stop, we would fill our saddlebags with dehydrated humus and tabouli. Tabouli, a Middle Eastern green salad, was particularly refreshing as produce was limited at the smaller shops along the way. Fresh teas and coffees were in there. There was oatmeal, jello, pancake mix and candy bars. Pasta had been separated into individual servings. Instant noodles were in there too. Jan had sent me a care package in Fort Nelson which contained homemade cookies, a rather long pepperoni, tuna fish, ramen noodles and vienna sausages. Along this section of road, Gary and I were eating well. We also had to carry a lot with us considering it was 330 miles from Fort Nelson to Watson Lake, Yukon, the next great population center with 1,700 residents. Fort Nelson had just over 3,000.

Peanut butter is the elixir of life on the road. We had stocked up on lots of it in Fort Nelson. However, the supply soon ran out. We found we would stop for coffee in a lodge, and mysteriously, the individual packets of peanut butter and jellies on the tables would disappear. Imagine that.

One thing that wasn't in the care packages was bread. Bread was something we ran out of quickly. We would often ask the lodges along the way to sell us a large loaf, and they always complied. It also seemed that every lodge had a baker who was skilled at creating the largest, most scrumptious cinnamon rolls known to creation. Quite often we would stop just to consume these roadside delicacies.

Gary was a skilled photographer. He would pull over to snap away at each interpretive sign. He also played the piano. His plan was to produce a slide show about his journey and write the music to it. This was the place to gather material.

Summit Lake, the highest point on the road at 4,250 feet, has some dramatic pyramid-shaped mountains rising over 7,000 feet above sea level. Pockets of winter's snow still clung to the gray rock even in the heat of summer as though winter would not release its deadly grasp. Treeline was there to almost touch. The mountains provided stunning backdrops for cycling and photos. The hilly terrain between Summit and a rushing river. Cycling along a river that is gushing the same way you are riding is a heady sensation. It is akin to walking up a moving escalator. Although the waters don't propel the rider forward, as an escalator does to a walker, it seems to do so. The water gives the sensation of speed. The crashing of the rapids against steady rock adds to nature's theater and the rider is treated to a wondrous play in which he is the star. The mountains dwarf you. The water cleanses. The rapids are applause. For several brief, wonderful moments, there is nothing else.

Where there is something, it comes in the form of wildlife. Stone sheep inhabit the roadside, playing and living in the jagged, rocky limestone gorge. They come out to the side of the road to play, eat and get photographed. They are used to people and the vehicles they drive. They aren't bothered by all the fuss.

Neither are some of the caribou that visit the side of the road by the park's exit. They, too, had seen people, even people on bicycles. Gary and I were able to stop, straddle our bicycles and just inch by the two caribou who hardly glanced our way. They didn't flinch as RV's went by. It was just another day at the feeding trough for these wild, tatty creatures tamed by man's hand-outs.

The emerald waters of Muncho Lake were next on this roller coaster ride. In 60 miles we had descended 2,000 feet, snaked through valleys, zipped down hills, crested others, been blinded by dust as the road sporadically would turn to dirt. We marvelled at nature's greenery. At times, the scene was more like an oil painting, created by a hand so huge it could not be comprehended. Yellow wildflowers lived in the grassy openings by the road. Trees with slender white trunks would tower above the thin, scrubby evergreens. Mountains rose from the earth, carpeted with green. Soon the carpet would run out, and the cragged, flat top of massive rock would reign high in the sky. Trickles of water would drop down from some spots. Scars from periods of heavy downpours blemished certain spots. No life would want to stand in the way of the rushing currents.

Muncho Lake was remote. A town of about 30 people, it has an airstrip just down the road from the Double "G" Service Station which doubled and tripled as a campground, motel, post office and cafe. Two and four seat planes waited by the gravel runway. A lone windsock served as a directional for the pilots.

For some reason that is hard to explain, even in the north and surrounded by mountains, Muncho Lake reminded me of the desert. The green/blue waters brought back memories of the Gulf of Eilat, the waterway with Jordan on one side and Israel on the other. Under those waters, I learned to dive. Now thousands of miles away and years later, by these waters, I cycled.

Cycle Gary and I did. We were going at a fairly good clip together. In the five days that we had been traveling together, we were averaging 52 miles per day. As a trip progresses and the body gets stronger, the time in the saddle changes. I thought back to the early days of New England and Ontario, how I wanted to be on the road just after the sun rose so I had the whole day to ride the 50 miles. Now, it seemed the riding time was down to between four and five hours for that same 50. To do more wasn't much of an effort.

But still, the body needed rewards for its work. Liard River Hot Springs called.

Locals say the best time to visit the hot springs at Liard River is in the dead of winter, when it's about 40 degrees below zero. Chances are you'll spot a moose as you cross the boardwalks leading to the two natural pools. You change in the rooms provided and dash quickly into the soothing waters. In the winter, there are no black flies, no mosquitoes, no overflowing parking lots and most importantly, no tourists.

But on the day Gary and I arrived, the steady stream of humans parading down the boardwalk in the rain to sample nature's treat made me long for winter. Soon humanity was forgotten as the healing waters massaged the body, reaching deep into the neck, shoulders, arms and legs. Man had constructed benches under the waters. Here we sat, conversed with others and enjoyed.

The campground full, we sought accommodations elsewhere. The likely spot was across the street at Trapper Ray's. The lodge was in the middle of an expansion. Bohemian-types sauntered about in tie-dye and long hair, digging, sawing and building. Activity was brisk. Business looked good for the trapper man. On a ladder was a young guy stuffing insulation between the logs of the new lodge. His baseball cap turned backwards, I could see a slight goatee on his chin. That hat looked familiar.

It was Matt.

Matt climbed down the ladder and was reunited with Gary. In a few minutes, we learned what had happened to Matt and Doug. They had gotten bored in Fort Nelson and bolted. No one seemed to care or acknowledge that in doing so, Matt and Doug had left Gary behind. Nonetheless, the pair had camped by the road as they had little money and existed on what meager food they had. At Trapper Ray's, Matt had gotten work. He was fed, paid cash and had a place to pitch his tent. He seemed happy.

There was a little friction between him and Doug. Doug had decided to press on by himself. The next mail drop was about 140 miles away in Watson Lake, Yukon. Apparently, Doug was a desperate dude.

Gary was also feeling some pressure at this point. His bicycle was giving him problems. Outside of Muncho Lake, he began having trouble shifting his gears. Instead of 21, he was now down to three. Considering this, he had been riding extremely well. He was grappling with continuing his ride or getting on the next bus back to anywhere but here.

We decided to head back across the street where the waters would make life seem a bit more clear.

Later, Gary tinkered with his rig. Matt tried too. So did a few other campers. No one could fix it. Gary decided to continue. Matt stayed behind.

We rode on.

With his bicycle hurting, Gary wanted to get to Watson Lake quickly. Doug was the master mechanic. Gary figured to catch up and let him operate on the bike. Less than 150 miles away, we figured we could get there in two days. With Watson Lake on our minds, the goal was clear — just get there. Ride like fire.

There are days that remind you of the joys and perils of long-distance bicycle touring. July 17th was one of those days.

Never before had the pace of bicycle travel been so graphically illustrated as to when a white Suzuki Sidekick travelling eastbound did a quick U-turn and then waited for me up ahead. Two figures got out of the car and stood by the road. As I got closer, and the figures became more focused, I recognized them as Simon and Phoebe.

They had driven from Toronto, Ontario and were heading out to Alaska and back in around three weeks.

Eleven days earlier we had met and had dinner together at the campground on Mile 17. They were now standing on the side of the road. In ground on Mile 17. They were now standing on the side of the road. In those 11 days, I traveled over 500 miles. In that time, they had driven through a wildfire, gotten to Alaska, looked around, saw the Portage Glacier, and were now on their way back home. The roadside meeting was brief. Simon showed me a cracked headlight on his vehicle and warned me about the construction between Whitehorse and the U.S. border.

Off they went.

Gary was doing remarkably well considering he had only three gears — tough, tougher and toughest. We were in some hilly terrain as the Yukon drew closer. Gary would muster as much speed as he could going down, but on those uphills, I would glance behind, and see him walking.

Poor Gary, I thought. Not even this mechanically-challenged male could help. Only company and encouragement could he offer.

There was a hiss that drowned out the thoughts.

Front flat tire.

Gary soon caught up and watched as I fixed the flat.

If there is any justice in the world, any great equalizer, it was in northern British Columbia that day. The flat fixed, on we went. Soon, around Coal River, there appeared a service station, the perfect place to top off the water bottles, rest and refresh. It was closed this particular Sunday, but the air pump outside didn't take the day off.

Eureka, this device would restore my hurt tube to maximum efficiency. I set the machine at 80 pounds per square inch, the maximum the tire would hold. In went the life-sustaining air as the bell from the pump chimed with each thrust.

That done, I leaned the bike against the building to go talk with Gary. Without warning, a gunshot echoed through the still day. I hit the ground.

I looked up to find Gary laughing and pointing to my rear tire.

"Dude, not good," he said.

No, it was not good. That gunshot sound was my rear tire. I had blown the thing beyond belief. A hole big enough for my index finger was now stationed in the sidewall of the tire. The tube had an even bigger hole.

There is an unspoken law of the road — self-sufficiency. Though you ride with someone, it is your responsibility to take care of yourself, your own problems. Now, I had a big one. I had no spare tire. That tube would take up my last patch. The nearest bike shop might as well have been on Mars. Gary offered me his spare tire, but it did not fit. He was down to only one patch. That would not be used.

New Englanders are known for their self-sufficiency. Ten years of my life has been spent living in Yankee country. A little of that Yankee ingenuity found its way into my blood. If there is one great fix-it in life, it is duct tape. The tape can hold everything together from cars to skis to jackets to sunglasses. That Sunday, it would save my tire.

The last patch went on the tube. Then the focus shifted to the tire. First, rubber cement was applied to the hole. Then the duct tape was skillfully wrapped around the hole. The tape covered both the outside, which would be in contact with the road, and the inside, which would be in contact with the tube.

We pressed on — the journey of the riding wounded.

Stress immediately returned to my life. Each revolution of the tire reminded me of this makeshift fix as the tape rubbed against the brake pads. Each revolution could have been the last.

Gary and I were transfixed on accumulating the miles. That day, we crossed over into the Yukon and made it to the Iron Creek Lodge after the kitchen had already closed. We gorged ourselves on ice cream after delirium set in during the last 10 miles or so over long, arduous hills that should never come at the end of a 100 mile day.

A shower and campsite never felt so welcomed.

The next day, I awoke to a flat tire. During the remaining 40 miles into Watson Lake, every few miles I would have to get off the bike and pump up the tire.

The campground in Watson Lake looked like a welcome friend. There was a payphone outside with a telephone book. The nearest bike shop was in Whitehorse, some 300 miles away.

Coleman Sinclair answered the phone at the Wheels and Brakes Cyclery and was listening to some incoherent ramblings from a cyclist who was near panic.

Don't worry he assured me, there's a bus to Watson Lake and we'll have a new tire, patch kit and two tubes on it. Just give me your credit card number.

I did.

The material arrived the next day. The stress left me. I later learned the bike shop gets around 50 calls a summer from riders in the Yukon who need parts shipped to them.

Gary found Doug who had been camping for free in the woods around Watson Lake. Doug had gotten his food from their prearranged mail drop, but his money still wasn't there. He wanted to wait a while. We could all use the rest. Gary needed to fix his bike, Doug wanted his cash, and I needed to transmit a story.

Doug wasn't having much fun. His girlfriend back in Montana had told him on the telephone she wanted to see someone else. Doug wanted to get home quickly, patch things up and have sex. So he and Matt parted ways. He figured Gary and I would eventually catch up with him.

We did.

Doug was able to temporarily fix Gary's bicycle. The derailleur wasn't able to shift properly due to a frayed cable. Doug shortened the cable, but Gary's relief was only for two or three days. The money Doug was waiting for in Watson Lake never came, so he worked out an arrangement with Gary to pay him back when the pair returned to Montana.

The three of us continued on, riding through some of the most pleasant terrain in the Yukon. One item missing from the landscape appeared to be power lines. At night, campers would fall asleep to the low hum of generators as those who lived between Forth Nelson, B.C. and Teslin, Yukon had to rely on themselves for power.

The Yukon was a place where romance met reality. The romance is on the mountain tops and in the aqua waters of the swift-running Yukon River. It's in the glow of the sun as it refuses to sink below the horizon until about midnight and in the sighting of a moose as it crosses the road to see what is on the other side. Purple fireweed frames every scenic photograph snapped off.

Reality is found in the stories of travelers. A New Jersey couple had been waiting nearly a week to repair the broken axle of their RV. It seems that every car with a Yukon license plate has a cracked windshield. Visitors tell of seized pistons in their engines and $50 Canadian oil changes. Motorcyclists complain of fast-flying gravel hitting their helmets and dashboards shorting out.

In the Yukon, it is said there are more moose than people. According to government statistics, nearly 32,000 hardy folks live in this northern place. Whitehorse is the largest city with 23,000. The next largest town is Dawson City with about 2,000 followed by Watson Lake with 1,815. There are 11 banks in the entire territory with five of them in Whitehorse. Grocery stores often serve as mall and bank. The Yukon is larger than New England and is not a place where you want to have a mechanical problem.

Gary was soon desperate. The quick fix wasn't working. In Teslin, population about 500, Gary called the Wheels and Brakes Cyclery. Coleman Sinclair listened and heard the babblings of a cyclist in near panic. He assured the rider the parts would be sent on the next bus from Whitehorse which would arrive the next day. What's your credit card number please?

Gary's problem ended, but soon it was Doug's turn. Doug was having trouble with one of his pedals. It was sticking and not properly turning. He took it apart. Inside there are ball bearings that allow the pedal to pedal. There are supposed to be about 20. Inside Doug's pedal were only three. He did not believe he could make it to Skagway with this pedal and cursed his fate by the side of the road.

As Gary and I did not carry spare pedals, Doug appeared to be screwed.

An RV with two bicycles on the back of it pulled over as Doug was letting fly a barrage of epithets, as sitting on the hot pavement of a road in the middle of nowhere with a broken pedal is not an ideal way to spend one's summer vacation. The kindly couple inquired as to the cyclist's predicament and Doug, remaining as calm as he could, explained. The couple then let Doug have one of the pedals from their bicycles.

Doug was saved.

But not his attitude about RV's. There is a love-hate relationship between bikers and RVers. It is mostly in the minds of the bikers though. Although RVers appear to be curious about these two-wheeling creatures, bikers can loathe these gas-guzzling, satellite dish-carrying, 500-mile-a-day traveling, octogenarian-operated roadhogs. The younger a rider is, the more they can't stand the RVers. Perhaps it is that they remind them of their parents who they definitely don't want to see when they are riding. Perhaps the RV stands for all they detest. A bicycle is the purest means of mechanical travel. The RV is a natural resource depleting machine. It carries with it what cyclists are seeking to escape.

The bicycle takes up little room on the road. The RV takes up too much. The biggest gripe seems to be that many RV's are operated by people who don't know what they are doing. At times, this is all too true. No special licenses are required for operating these mega-horsepower creations. Often these people don't know where they are going. The driver looks at the sights by the road while his wife has the VCR out recording the voyage. This can be most disconcerting. Also, RVer's play drag racers sometimes. A bicyclists heart stops as he rounds the curve and finds two mechanical mammoths approaching on a two-lane road.

But just as there are good people and bad people, not all RVer's are bad. I once thought like Doug, that RVer's are sent from hell. But that has changed. They are adventurers in their hearts. Many have chosen the road as their home, bypassing God's waiting room which Americans refer to as Florida. For many, the RV is their only home. All their lives they have worked, paid off the house and put their children through school. It is their turn to explore and see the world. As one RVer once told me: "We hit the road so our children would stop moving back home."

RVer's are a source of information. They will gladly top off your water bottles. On a hot day, one can find cool shade near their bellies. They feed you, console you and offer companionship. They provide beer on a warm day and one even did our dishes as we had an impromptu lunch by the roadside.

And as Doug found out that day, they can save you when you are miles from nowhere.

Jake's Corner is a crossroads. The Alaska Highway continues west while travelers can pick up the Klondike Highway heading south to the American border and Alaska.

At Jake's Corner, I said good-bye to Doug and Gary. After all their misadventures, it was a good two weeks of fun.

This spot was also a special place for me. Alaska was only a day away had I continued to travel with the pair. When I started the trip, I had planned to make a decision at Jake's Corner — stop or continue. Alaska is so vast, that here was an opportunity for me to end the trip. After all, the trip was to go from Maine to Alaska. I rejoiced being alone once again. I thought how my fears had gone, how life was reduced to finding food, shelter and fixing any bike problems (or finding someone who could). It was here that I knew I would be able to continue on to the

Pacific Ocean, and cross a continent from sea to sea.

The next day, Gary was hit by an RV on the Klondike Highway nearly 15 miles from his final destination of Skagway. Doug and Gary were ascending White Pass, the final climb to 3,290 feet. From there, it was to be a cyclist's dream. About 12 miles downhill to Skagway and the Tayla Inlet of the Pacific Ocean.

The two were in sort of a no man's land between the two countries. Canadian customs was behind them and they had yet to go through American customs.

For what seemed like hours, they inched up the Klondike. It was windy and the two were tired.

As they neared the top, Gary was struck by a recreational vehicle.

"Gary went flying. His bike was trashed and I was freaking out," recalled Doug.

A Canadian government pick-up truck was passing by and took the two riders and their equipment into Skagway. According to Doug, "the two old farts in the RV, I think from Michigan, wouldn't even drive him to the hospital." Gary was treated and released from the hospital. He had sprained his ankle and had some abrasions.

The two did not seek work. They stayed in Skagway for about a week and then took a ferry to Washington, rented a car there and drove to Vancouver where they hopped on a bus to Seattle. They got on another bus to Boseman, Montana and then hitched back to West Yellowstone from there. Doug, of course, borrowed the money for all this from Gary and did pay him back. He and his girlfriend did not patch things up.

When they got home, Frank was already back and had set up camp in some woods. He had cycled back from Pink Mountain, British Columbia.

Matt also eventually made it back to West Yellowstone. He worked at Trapper Ray's for a few more weeks, but his bicycle was in bad shape with a bottom bracket shot. He met a pair of Irish girls and traveled with them to Denali National Park, Alaska. They eventually dropped him off in Skagway where he got a job washing dishes, saved some money, headed back to Atlanta and then back to West Yellowstone.

All four trolls made it home.

Romance Meets Reality

On the floor of Jeff and Trish Dorn's red Bronco was an empty pack of Player cigarettes. Scrawled on it were the words: "Stuck in hell with no way out — Fort Nelson, B.C. July 14, 1994." Trish wrote those words.

It was supposed to have taken the young couple about 10 days to drive the 2,480 miles from Thompson, Manitoba to Whitehorse, Yukon. Jeff had just taken a job as a television producer and the two were looking forward to Yukon life.

But a broken clutch left them stranded for five days in Fort Nelson as they waited for the parts to be sent to them from Edmonton, Alberta over 1,000 miles away. The parts did come — the wrong parts. So they had to be ordered from another place.

The Dorns eventually made it to Whitehorse on a Saturday and Jeff started his job that Monday. I met the Dorns in Fort Nelson, BC. They had given me Jeff's work number and told me to look them up in Whitehorse.

"You can stay with us," said Jeff. "Unless you make it there before us. Then we'll have to stay with you."

The Dorns made it there first. However, the travel delay made it difficult for them to find a home as Jeff started work immediately and Trish found a job too. Luckily, they had some friends who lived on Main Street — Rich and Eileen. There was room in the backyard for the Dorns to pitch a tent and there they lived with their two dogs. It was there I set up my tent and spent a few days in Whitehorse.

There is nothing like visiting a town and being hosted by locals, even if they are locals for a few days. They know the bars, restaurants and sights to see. They know the back roads and places that aren't in the tour guides. If you do want to go to the mainstream places, they'll get you there off-peak to avoid the masses.

Here was chance for me to get back into civilization for a day or so while still sleeping out during the starless summers of the Far North. Eileen tended bar at the Kopper King, so that was a stop. Trish was a waitress at one of the hotels. That was a stop. Jeff took me over to the offices of where he worked for a glimpse of his efforts. Hot summers called for swimming. Whitehorse has a rather long swimming hole right in town — Miles Canyon. The waters flow quickly but there are spots that tame the current and invite swimming. The Whitehorse Rapids Fishway was a place to wait for salmon that were about to make their annual run to the spawning grounds, but that was still a few days away. The MacBride Museum, downtown on First Avenue, showed the history of the Yukon from prehistoric times to the coming of the telegraph during the Gold Rush Days.

But the most memorable visit during my stay in Whitehorse was to the movies. "Forrest Gump" was playing, the box office smash of the summer. Starring Tom Hanks, it told the hilarious and incredible story of a man with a low IQ becoming a millionaire and falling in love.

Gump became a celebrity due to his rapid rise in the business world. His movement were well-documented in the media. Snubbed by the woman he loved, Gump started to run. He ran and ran. Gump ran from one end of America to the other. He developed a following. People ran with him. He got to the other side of America. He still felt like running. He turned around and started to run back. This continued for two years.

One day he was running over a bridge. The media waited for him and began hounding him with questions. They wanted to know why Gump was going this. Maybe it was for cancer victims or AIDS research or some other pious reason. Not loosing a step, Gump spoke into the microphones thrust into his face.

"I just feel like running," he said.

Well, I just felt like biking.

Through the wild Yukon I went, creeping further north. This was a time I did a lot of riding alone. Other bicycling tourists were starting to come out, but they all were coming from the other way. Many were from Europe, particularly Germany and Switzerland. They would fly to

Anchorage, and start their eastward trek there. Several would also head north, up to Dawson City and even up to Inuvik, on the Dempster Highway and in the Northwest Territories. There were a few top to bottom riders as well. These were folks going from Alaska to Chile. They would start at Prudhoe Bay, Alaska, the furthest point north in the state that is accessible by road and cycle thousands of miles to Tierra Del Fuego in Chile, land's end. There were a few cycling the Alaska Highway, one going from Alaska to Guatemala and a few traveling from Alaska, down the Cassiar Highway in British Columbia to Prince Rupert where they would catch a ferry for a magnificent ride on the Marine Highway.

Signs became my friends. They were mileposts, telling what was ahead and if I turned my head around and looked on the other side of the road, what was behind. The mind drifted back to places like upstate New York where my favorite sign told of a store that advertised "groceries, gas, guns, guitars." Ontario was a place with some winners. One chain of gasoline stations was called "Major Gas." This was particularly funny after a meal of rice and beans. "Latchford, the best little town near a dam site" was another favorite. The signs separating the Arctic and Atlantic watersheds were a pleasure to see as I had never seen a river flow north before. Manitoba had an interesting sign that said "Orbit...10 secs." On the Yellowhead Highway were egg-shaped trash receptacles. The sign would indicate to a motorist he was roughly 10 seconds from the barrel. Neepawa looked like it had some interesting characters around. Although all I did was stop for a meal, I did see some funny ones. There was a hog slaughtering plant, so a sign outside it said hogs, receiving. The town is also the purple martin capital of the world and declared itself so on tower with 15 birdhouses. Entering the town, a sign said, "Welcome and Bienvenue to Neepawa. Population 996,600 Short of One Million. If You Can't Stop Smile As You Go By."

I couldn't help but smile as I rode through the Yukon. Each waterway seemed to have a name, now matter how small it seemed. One creek was named "No Name Creek." Travelers were welcomed to the community of Destruction Bay with a bulldozer at each end of town. A town you are unlikely to find on a map is Stephenville. A hand-crafted sign declared the name of the town and "Pop. 7, including Mom."

The community of Burwash Landing had a gigantic gold pan to honor those who came in search of nature's treasure in front of the local museum. But the sign that stayed with me for some time was one that came

Construction was an obstacle for every vehicle making the pilgrimage along the Alaska Highway. Trucks were so massive, drivers needed ladders to reach the steering wheel. (Photo by Marty Basch).

about 100 miles from the United State border — "Rough Road Next 165 km. Max. Recommended Speed 70 km/h." Word roamed the highway that this last section of road in Canada was the worst on the entire highway. Natural deterioration and huge frost heaves tore up the road in 1993 and reconstruction was planned for the summer of 1994, seems to mean tear up the road and build a new one.

The pavement turned to gravel. At times I wondered what RV's were doing on my mountain bike trail. It was on sections like this that one understood why windshields get cracked, axles get broken and tires become flat. Luckily I was on fat tires as the rubber would sink into the dirt. At least I had traction. Skinny-tired cyclists were probably cursing their decision.

Every once in a while traffic would come to a halt. There would be a worker with a stop sign holding up the procession as monster earth-moving trucks needed room to pass. On some sections, these trucks would come within inches of me. But I was on a bicycle and invincible, right? They would see me coming on my purple rig, right?

So it was quite a shock when I got to the front of the halted traffic and waited for the sign to be switched from stop to slow.

"Just a second. We'll put you in the pilot truck," said the holder of the sign.

"Huh?"

"You think you can ride through this. Uh-uh. You're going in the back."

"Yeah, but I've pedaled here from Maine."

"In the back."

Within seconds, I found myself lifting my bicycle and gear into the back as people got out of their vehicles and took pictures. The mandatory ride lasted only about a mile. The construction companies, for insurance reasons, did not allow bicyclists to ride through certain work sites as the machinery is too big and often the drivers can't see a speck on the ground at the top of a rig they have to climb a ladder to get into.

This happened one more time during this rough stretch of road.

Serious construction is one obstacle bikers aren't allowed to tackle on the Alaska Highway. There is another one too — wildfires.

Jinkzie Green Revisted

For six days, Jinkzie Green traveled in John Hedden's panniers from the Yukon to Sitka, Alaska. Hedden and his traveling companion, Joanne Harrison, stopped at the border to enter the United States.

The guards asked if they had anything to declare, as bringing a dead person from one country to another is something the country the dead person is visiting would like to know.

"I didn't mention her," said Hedden, recalling the event..

Jinkzie then spent most of August in Hedden's place as he waited for the right day to scatter her ashes on Harbor Mountain in Sitka.

On September 10th, Hedden decided the day had come. He and a friends got on their mountain bikes and pedaled up to a nice place with a good view of town, the mountains and ocean. Hedden opened the envelope and let Jinkzie fly into the wind.

"I told her to enjoy Sitka and I hoped that she enjoyed the ride," he said.

On the other side of the world in New Hampshire, a reporter for *The Conway Daily Sun* was at work on a story. Seems a colleague of his was biking across Canada and came upon a bicycling couple carrying the remains of a dead woman. He wrote a column about the two-wheeled procession through the Yukon and that story appeared in the newspaper.

The next thing you know, the newspaper got a telephone call from a woman named Louise Lovell. She lives in the small town of Freedom with her husband, Clement. Their son Joe was reading the exploits of the Sun's peripatetic correspondent when he remarked that those people traveling in the RV sounded a lot like his sister and brother-in-law. He gave the article to his mom Louise and she read it.

"These people aren't like Marla and Ron, they are Marla and Ron," she said.

Marla called the Lovell's once a week during her journey. She never mentioned Jinkzie. Imagine her surprise when she telephoned and her family back home knew about her wilderness experience.

"That's some circuitous route for information to travel," Joe told the newspaper.

No doubt Jinkzie (whose real name is Jennie) would have loved all this attention.

So This is Alaska

On August 2 at 10:51 a.m. Yukon Standard Time, 4,333 miles from Portland, Maine and three months to the day after starting from the Atlantic coast, I crossed the border back into the USA and into Alaska.

There was no band, no parade, no fireworks. The wind still blew and the sun continued to beat down upon the land as if nothing had happened.

There were two welcome signs, the flags of the U.S. and Canada, an international boundary marker and a few placards detailing the history of the Alaska Highway. Two German tourists were there as well. They took my picture.

Crossing the border was effortless. After answering a few questions, I was back in the land of green money.

That was it.

The same thing happened a few days later at Delta Junction, the end of the Alaska Highway. After 1,422 miles on that road, a sign signified the end of the road. No fanfare there either.

If there is a lesson to be learned while bicycle touring it is that the destination isn't important. It's the journey that matters. That's where the challenges are, the scenery, the people and the serendipity.

So through Alaska I go. Tok, about 100 miles into the 49th state, is a town which seems to survive with tacky ways of separating tourists from their dollars. A nightly sled dog demonstration is seemingly nothing but a way to get people into the store by which it is held so they buy lots of things. The entertainment at a local gas station/restaurant/RV park featured people in cowboy hats doing line dances to rap music. That seems demographically impossible.

Onward I went. The hordes of mosquitoes people talked about are a reality. So are grasshoppers. They lined the road and would jump out of the way as I rode by. Some would hop on my saddlebags, ankles, thighs and shoes. Others weren't too bright. They tried to escape through the spokes of my wheel and were decapitated.

There are lots of yellow jackets. But these bees aren't so bad. They just hang around while you cook outdoors and play games of psychological terror, circling you, yet not stinging. At least not yet.

Then there are the no-see-um's. I can see um. They are in the hairs on my arms, the nape of my neck and on my forehead. They wait for you, hovering over the pavement and then attack. The bugs can even sneak into your mouth or up your nose. Yuk!

Smoke also creeps through the olfactory senses. The smoke comes from wildfires that burn each summer in the vast wilderness outside of towns. There are days when the smoke of burning fires creates a haze across the land. It can be seen and smelt for miles. The fires burn for days, weeks. That is the philosophy for fighting fires. Let them burn as part of nature's way to rejuvenate itself. The scars of the fires are frequent. Outside of Tok, trees are still blackened from the burn of 1990. That fire ate up nearly 100,000 acres. It threatened the town. Roads had to be closed.

There was a growing haze August 4th as the miles put Tok behind me. The haze grew past the tiny hamlet of Dot Lake and continued to come closer until a man with a radio stopped traffic outside a bridge. The smoke looked like it was just miles down the road.

"Can I ride through it?," I asked the man, my invincibility and stupidity shining through. It didn't matter that a campground up ahead was closed because of the approaching fire or that the road had been shut for a few hours each day because of the fire. No, I wanted to ride through.

"I'll ask," he said.

The voice on the other end of the radio said, "Negative."

I knew the routine and waited for the pilot vehicle.

From the back of a pick-up truck, the fire didn't look too bad. There was smoke and flames shooting 20 or 30 feet from the road. How bad could it be if they were letting cars drive through? Nonetheless, safety came first and I was able to use both hands to steady the camera as I clicked away.

Alaskans also love things with motors. Since it's so dark in the winter with hardly any sunlight, they make up for it in the summer with long days beyond midnight. All up and down rivers, they ride loud, powerful boats. At 2 a.m. you can hear the airboats zipping down the Salcha River as they shake the tent. Around midnight, jet skis are still whopping it up on the Chena in Fairbanks.

Yes, Alaskans love the outdoors. The pleasant bike paths around Fairbanks — the city with a golden heart — are filled with bikers and bladers. Hell, there's even a winter bike race called the Iditasport where diehards cycle 160 miles in sub-zero weather. With the Tanana Valley Fair in town, Alaskans stay outdoors, riding the rides, gorging themselves on fried foods and entertaining themselves with shows from hypnotists to marionettes.

There are concerts, art festivals and a university high on top of a hill with an excellent museum that's a little small. You can actually camp in the city limits and there's even an animal research station in this city of maybe 70,000 that has musk ox, reindeer and caribou. There's even minor league baseball up here. And yes, there is a town called the North Pole. It's just outside Fairbanks.

Alaskans refer to the rest of the country as the Lower 48, with the exception of Hawaii of course. Then there's a strange phrase — the Outside — that permeates the media. This, I think, refers to every place else in the world but here. Sounds a bit egotistical, but you could understand the isolation Alaskans may feel.

And I don't know who started this 10 men to one woman ratio here, but that's malarkey. Maybe it's that way in villages with no roads in the middle of the bush, but not here. No, I'm happy to report that the ample scenery around here can make a biker miss a stop sign or two. Yup, there seems to be enough lycra to go around.

The one thing though that sticks out here is the friendliness. This was told to me by a few people I have never met. Carrying a laptop computer on this trip, I have been fortunate enough to have people send me e-mail from two countries who have been reading my columns in a number of places. A number of folks have written me how the further north I would go, the friendlier people would get.

There I was, no more than 10 minutes in Fairbanks after completing the Alaska Highway on August 6 and already I'm cursing the one-way streets all going the wrong way. I was waiting for the light to change at Peger and Airport Way when a bicycling man with a bandanna on his head stopped and looked right at me: "Hey, I've been reading your articles."

That's the best complement a writer can get, and it's also how I met Johnny Dickey, a geophysicist for the U.S. Geological Survey in Fairbanks. Dickey was a recent transplant to Alaska. He was a reader of *The Fairbanks News-Miner*. Each week he read the exploits of "Rodeman." The paper carried a photograph of me with the articles. Dickey recognized me from it and invited me in. That's friendly.

So here I am in Dickey's apartment on the banks of the Chena, thankful for a break in last week's record 90-plus heat and watching the sun shine on the geraniums lining the deck while two cats named Dweeb and Pud sleep in the shade. It is the first time I'll be sleeping inside for a month. So this is Alaska.

Denali

Bear Meets Biker

Denali means many things to many people. The Tanana Indian name means the "high one." At 20,320 feet, it is the highest peak in North America. For climbers, it is a mecca, one that calls the challenge.

Others call the rock pile Mt. McKinley. It is one in the same. Alpinists die climbing the peak. Nearly 1,000 people make the annual pilgrimage to climb it between April and June.

Those who climb, come face to face with themselves. The elements can prove savage and deadly. At 16,000 feet, fierce winds howling at over 100 miles per hour can rip a tent apart, forcing skilled mountaineers to dig snowcaves. Ravens are said to hover over camps, waiting to scavenge food left behind. Located between Fairbanks and Anchorage, Denali National Park is one of the most visited, if not the most visited, spot in Alaska. It's a damn zoo.

The zoo begins miles outside the park. Coming from Fairbanks, the banks of the Nenana River are lined with tents and recreational vehicles. Inside these said items are people waiting to get inside the park. They want to see the mighty mountain. They want to see a caribou. They want to see a grizzly bear. The human zoo on the outside of the park continues. Restaurants, hotels, tour operators and grocery stores all bid for the dollar. There is a rush for accommodations. They rush for food. Rush, rush, rush.

The dollars come from all over. There are Canadians. Maybe those are Germans. Hey, is that Hebrew? Those folks over there could be from Japan. That sounds like Spanish. They fly, from all over the world to come to the Great Land. Many spend hours on the plane. They land in

Anchorage. Then, they hop on a tour bus to the park. At the park, they get on another tour bus to go into the park and see the animals.

If the weather is clear, they smile. Oh, look at their cameras — big ones, short ones, expensive ones, cheap ones. There's a caribou. They take a picture. There's a grizzly bear. Better get a picture. Are those white dots up there Dall sheep? Better get a picture. Chances are, they are just hikers with white shirts.

If the weather isn't cooperating, they frown. When you're dealing with a mountain four miles high, clouds can get in the way and even the most expensive video camera can't make them go away. They listen to a lecture, spend a night at a hotel, and then get on another tour bus to see another part of the land called Alaska.

For me, Denali means only one thing — grizzly bear.

The mayhem upon first entering the park can be exaggerated for a cyclist used to the solitude of the road. Denali is a popular destination and those without reservations for campsites are forced to wait until a site becomes available. On August 13th, I entered the park and waited in line with all the others who had come from afar. My plan was cycle the 86-mile Park Road to Wonder Lake Campground. I needed to get a camping spot along the road and at Wonder Lake.

I was able to make a reservation for the 14th at the Teklanika River Campground at mile 29 on the road and on the 15th for Wonder Lake. The beauty of Denali is that it welcomes and rewards those who get there on their own power or who plan to take multi-day excursions into the backcountry. There is a campground inside the park about a mile or so from the entrance called Morino that is reserved for hikers and bikers. No one is turned away. It was a primitive looking place — a few toilets, water taps and picnic tables. Showers could be purchased for a couple of dollars at a store across the road.

Here, backcountry hikers would wait for their turn to head into the taiga and tundra. These were not the people waiting to climb the peak. They were heading into the wilderness for a few days. Each party was assigned a particular section of the park and it is there they would explore. They carried their own water, their own food. The food, so as not to alert grizzly bears, was carried in what the park service called BRFC's. That stands for Bear Resistant Food Containers. Basically, they are hard black containers that bears aren't supposed to be able to open. It contains the odors so bears can't smell any pepperoni sticks. The toothpaste

The Park Road in Denali winds and snakes through four mountain passes. Most of the visitors are transported into the park via yellow school buses. Mt. McKinley is in the distance, partially hidden by clouds. (Photo by Marty Basch).

and deodorant go in there, too. If it could attract a bear, it went in there.

All food, dirty cooking containers and items with odors like toiletries had to be kept in food storage lockers located in the park's campgrounds. These are huge, brown metal shacks. Bears could not open them. Sometimes humans couldn't open them either. The doors squeaked loudly with each swing of the door. The handle was a loop one had to twist in order to open and close. Friendships were made when a person would call for help to open the things.

In the backcountry, visitors just hiked with maps. There were no trails aside from a few walking paths near the entrance. Those waiting to take their Denali adventure would speculate on their plans. Those coming back would rest at Morino and entertain the newcomers with tales. Information was exchanged. Acquaintances were made across picnic tables. Two subjects dominated conversation — the weather and bears.

August can mean cold and rain in a land where there is a mountain four miles high. A forecast of rain drains the smiles. Rain means clouds and they obscure the mountain. Everyone wants to see the "high one".

Everyone also wants to see a grizzly bear. Denali is a 6,000,000 acre preserve and home to a few hundred grizzly bears. Grizzly bears are big. The female can weigh around 300 pounds while the male tips the scales at an average of 500 pounds. Just because they are big, doesn't mean they are slow. These creatures can run faster than 30 miles per hour.

Grizzlies also like to eat. Berries in August are a favorite. They are sweet and plentiful. Eighty percent of their diet is vegetation. So the remaining twenty percent is meat. They can choose from many types of meat in the preserve. There is moose, caribou, ptarmigan, fox, wolf, porcupine and Dall sheep. Apparently these prove tasty to the grizzly.

One other source of meat is human. With thousands of visitors to the park each year, odds are that a human will meet a bear. There has yet to be a human death in the park attributed to the grizzly bear, and park rangers are out to make sure that doesn't happen.

Bear safety is top priority in Denali. Go to a lecture and a ranger will tell you what to do if you meet a grizzly bear. Read the park newspaper and there are instructions on how to avoid an encounter. It tells readers what to do if you happen to meet up with Yogi and friends.

To avoid an encounter, first be alert. Look for their tracks and scat. Try not to surprise a bear, especially a mother and cub. Surprise can be perceived as a threat. In the backcountry, sing or shout. This alerts the bear to your presence. Finally, never approach a bear.

Let's say you do all these things or the bear is just in a playful mood. Maybe they actually like your singing and want to encourage more. If you encounter a bear, the park suggests a few ways to stay alive. The first is don't run. If the bear is unaware of you, just quietly get out of there. That's simple.

Should the bear be aware of you, that is something entirely different. You shouldn't run because that might trigger a chase response from the bear and chances are the bear is faster than you are. Instead, stop and put your arms over your head. Wave them. Then, in a low, calm voice talk to the bear. Slowly, back away.

Okay, you're doing this, but the bear isn't impressed and wants to take a closer look. Stand still. Sometimes the bear will make a bluff charge and stop 10 feet from a person.

If the bear appears to get ready to charge, drop down into a human ball and play dead. Odds are the bear will sniff around and then go

Wildlife is frequently seen in Denali National Park. Tourists snap away at the Dall sheep, moose, bears and caribou. These caribou were having lunch by the Eielson Visitor Center. (Photo by Marty Basch).

home. Apparently, bears stink. The stench can be overwhelming. Be cool.

Should all this fail and the bear decides to have you for dinner, the park has the following advice, culled from the *Denali Alpenglow* newspaper: "If the attack is prolonged, change tactics and fight back vigorously."

I was ready to roll.

Seeing Denali by bicycle is seeing a piece of heaven. First glimpse of a caribou while in the saddle is like holding a newborn. Round a corner and there is McKinley, a massive snow-encrusted jewel. Marvel at the creation in nature. Riding with the evening sun as it lights up the tops of the Alaska Range makes any rider forget the clouds of dust he has encountered by vehicles along the way. The tundra is rolled out before you, a carpet where nature's game of life and death is played.

When there is silence, imagination takes over. Distant rocks become bears. Hikers with t-shirts are Dall sheep. Any leaf, any scrub bush that the wind rustles can cause the heart to stop briefly.

Solitude is broken by yellow school buses. In it are tourists looking for wildlife. They leave the park entrance and take an eight hour round trip bus ride to a visitor center at the 66 mile mark. Along the way, they look for wildlife. The drivers are jovial. They keep one eye on the narrow, twisting, roller coaster of a road and the other on the taiga and tundra in search of animals. The visitors are also searching. Over 150 eyes scan through the trees, the mountains and the roadside, wanting to see nature's beauty. One sees movement in the distance. The driver is alerted. The bus is pulled over. There is a rush to one side of the bus. Lenses face the movement. Binoculars peer at the horizon. "There it is," someone cries. One by one each visitor sees what it is to see. Sometimes it is a caribou. Sometimes a grizzly bear is there. Often, these animals appear as specks and only the most powerful of lenses can see them. Other times, the animals cross in front of the bus. When they do, there is a rush to the front of the bus, or to the rear. This is but one way to see the park.

The park road starts as pavement. Just 15 miles into the ride, the road crosses the Savage River and enters another dimension. Vehicular traffic becomes limited. The road turns to dirt. The views become limitless.

There are times of silence, and then there is dust. Buses pass by, courteous of the rider. A friendly wave comes from the driver and the assembled. The bus passes slowly. In its' wake, it leaves dust. The rider eats the dust, curses the bus and continues. There are times the buses travel in teams. One, two and three pass by. The rider waits on a road with no shoulder. A thin layer of dirt cakes the body. A bandanna covers the mouth. It filters the air. When a trio of buses pass the rider is transported to the Sahara. It is hot, sticky. The 29 miles are done. Four mountain passes are ahead. Rest.

Fifty- seven miles are on the agenda for Monday, August 15th. Just 57 miles to Wonder Lake. Between Teklanika and the campground are a number of passes. There are: Sable Pass at 3,900 feet, Polychrome Pass at 3,700 feet, Highway Pass at 3,980 feet and Thorofare Pass at 3,900 feet. Guard rails are unheard of out here. The road can only accommodate one bus at a time. One pulls over, the other passes. Then the other goes. Those looking out from their bus windows at certain passes, just look down into a chasm of nothing for hundreds of feet.

I ride. There are the damn buses, yellow and brown ones. Go away. Stop choking me.

It's been a few miles. One pulls over up ahead. It pulls to the right. When a bus stops, the rider stops. That is a sure sign of wildlife.

A tourist with a long-lensed camera leans out from a window on the right side of the bus as I approach.

"Grizzly," he says.

"Where," I say.

"Up there. By that ridge," he answers.

He hands me the camera. I peer through the lens. I see hills, bush, nothing else.

"Don't see it," I say.

"Look hard," he says.

I look harder. Something moves. It's a grizzly bear. I'm on bike. There's a grizzly bear. It was hundreds of yards away. That was good.

I return the camera.

The yellow bus parade continues. Soon, it comes to halt.

One, two, three buses are on the road. The buses tilt to the left. That means wildlife is over there, across the road.

A woman sticks her head out from the left side of the bus.

"Grizzly," she says. "You better go around."

I stick my neck out as far as it could go. There about 100 feet away on the other side of the road was a grizzly. He was eating berries. I felt like a meal on wheels.

Immediately, I head for the right side of the bus, get off my bike and use the bus as a blocker.

The driver opens the door.

"Get in. You need some protection," he says.

I comply. I smile at the tourists. For a second, I am more of a curiosity than the bear. They return to watching the bear eat. So do I. It is a nonstop eating machine. I'm glad I'm in the bus.

Then the driver tells me to get out. He's got a schedule to keep and there's no room for me and the bike.

You're kidding, my expression must have said.

The driver opened the door.

Two buses are ahead. I exit the bus. I get my camera out from the handlebar bag. It is in my right hand. In my left hand I have the bicycle.

The plan is to make a dash for the two other buses and snap a photograph to show my friends. There isn't much time to think. I'm off and running. The camera snaps away. I make it to one bus. The buses are now moving. I run along the side. Not so fast guys. Take your time. From bus number two I hurry to bus number one. Maybe the driver sees me. He seems to slow down. I run along the side. He leaves some dust. Bus two passes. It leaves dust. I'm still running. The third bus passes. The dust tastes better than death.

The bear never saw me.

Focus returns to the road. I see caribou. I see hikers. I see 36 miles ahead of me with hairpin turns, curves, steep drop-offs and oh-so-thin sections. It is largely uphill.

I frequently stop to rest. The road is very steep in sections. But the views are tremendous. Highway Pass, the highest pass on the highway, is splendid. From it, Denali is seen. It is almost in your face. There is some cloud cover, but it sparkles. It is life. The effort increases the beauty of the view. The smile is as wide as the mountain is high.

The road goes on forever here. You see it for miles. It snakes to the horizon. Then the horizon ends and there is the fourth pass. Thorofare Pass is crested.

Just over a mile later is the Eielson Visitor Center. There is water and exhibits. Caribou come near the center. Tourists can almost touch them. They take pictures. Some stupid people try to get too close. The rangers come out. They tell the stupid people to move back.

The north and south peaks of Denali make a most excellent backdrop. There are glaciers. It is glorious.

Wonder Lake is only 20 miles away. I'm told by a ranger the ride is mostly downhill from here. I smile.

Life is good. The sun is shining. The body is strong. It is time to move on.

The views, oh the views. Down deep to the left is the tundra. There is the Alaska Range. The bicycle picks up speed. There are no more yellow buses. The dust is forgotten. One mile goes by.

The smile is contagious. The road is filled with turns. Up and down I go. I am alone. Another half mile goes by. The wind breezes past me. I round a corner.

Time stops. I slam on the brakes.

There is a grizzly bear about 75 feet from me.

There are no more yellow buses. No more dust. There are no more park rangers. There is just silence. But my ears are ringing. It is my heart, beating, beating, beating.

The grizzly is light brown in color. Its rippling muscle and fat creep closer. It senses me and keeps coming on all fours.

Slowly, ever so slowly, I get off my bike. I put it down by the side of the road. Slowly, so slowly, the arms go over the head and start to cross.

I spoke to the bear.

"Good bear. Damn good bear. You're the best bear," I say in a low, moderate tone, attempting to hide the terror inside.

The bear labors forward. Was it taking an interest in me? Did it smell the food in my packs? I didn't have a BRFC. Life is in slow motion. My legs start to move backwards.

To the right is rock. To the left is a sheer straight drop-off. This seems like forever. Where are the buses? Please, some vehicle come by. Distract the bear. How far back will I have to walk? Will I have to curl up into a human ball and let the bear play with me? I don't think I can take it.

"Good bear, good bear," I say. Is this 10 seconds, 20 seconds, a minute?

A pick-up truck rounds the corner. There is the truck, the bear, the bicycle and me. The bear appears to go for my food-laden packs. The pick-up inches forward. It nudges the bear. The bear scampers down the cliff.

I fall to my knees.

I thank my maker.

Life is good.

A man and woman stepped from the pick-up truck and walked towards the kneeling figure.

"You wouldn't happen to have a shot of whiskey," I asked.

The man said no.

I started to get up and noticed the blood on my knees from kneeling.

"Are you okay?," the woman asked.

"I'm a bit shaky," I answered.

The man and woman introduced themselves as Jeff and Wendy. They were kind. They helped me get my bike back up. They suggested they turn their pick-up around and follow me for a mile or so to make sure the bear wouldn't come back. He knew about grizzly bears. Jeff showed me his arms. He still had the scars from when he was mauled by a grizzly eight years ago in Glacier National Park, Montana.

"I know how you feel," he said. "That's one scary experience."

They followed me for a mile or so. By then, I had stopped shaking.

I was alone again. Each shadow now looked like a bear. Each curve was frightening. Was there another one?

I heard a sound. I stopped.

"Hey bear, hey bear," I heard. I looked down into the distance. There were a pair of hikers going through the bush. They were making sounds to fend off bears.

Finally vehicles came again. I flagged down one with a government seal on it. I told the man about the bear. I told him about Jeff and Wendy.

"Oh I know Jeff and Wendy," he said. "Jeff's brother is Dave. He's the postmaster here in the park. I think they're visiting from New Hampshire."

The Wonder Lake campground never looked so good. Nearly at the end of civilization as modern man knows it, Wonder Lake is a place for tents only. The ground looks upon Denali.

That night I watched the moon over Denali in the land of the midnight sun. I saw the sun's rays touch so softly upon Denali and the other peaks in a concert of alpenglow. Other campers sat on picnic tables and watched, transfixed. The moon rose. It started on one side of the mountain and slowly made its way across the sky. There were whispers. Camera shutters clicked.

The moon soon hid behind the peaks.

The day was done.

It was August 16th and I was in the post office in Denali. To get there, I had taken the bus from Wonder Lake. I was still a little bear-shy.

I met Jeff's brother and he arranged for Jeff to swing by. I wanted to thank him again.

"We came around the corner and saw the bear first and then the bicycle," Jeff recalled. "We assumed you ran uphill. We saw the bear moving towards the bike and drove to the bear. Then we saw you. The idea was to keep the packs away from the bear. It got trickier when we saw you. We didn't want to push the bear back to you."

If the bear had gotten to the packs, it might learn to associate bicyclists with food. Jeff pointed out the bear might have been confused too, stuck between the pick-up and a human.

It wasn't a fun time for either bear or human.

"It's terrifying. I've been in that situation," Jeff said.

We recalled the event. Wendy even had a camera next to her in the pick-up. Jeff had encouraged her to take photos, but Wendy balked at the idea. Apparently, I looked somewhat frightened.

"So, I hear you're from New Hampshire," I said to Jeff after a while.

"So am I. Where are you from?"

"Jackson," he said.

"Jackson? That's incredible. I'm from North Conway," I said. North Conway and Jackson, New Hampshire are less than 10 miles away from each other.

"Hey, do you read *The Conway Daily Sun?*" I asked Jeff.

"Sure," he said.

"You wouldn't happen to be following that guy who's riding his bike to Alaska?,"

"Oh yeah. I've been reading it all summer. What's his name? Marty Basch or something."

I stuck out my hand.

"Pleased to meet you," I said.

Jeff Brown and Wendy Zug are married. That August they were visiting family and friends as Brown had once worked in Denali. Now, Brown was employed as the hut system manager at the Appalachian Mountain Club in Pinkham Notch, New Hampshire. It is a place I had lectured at several times. It is 16 miles from my house.

Wendy Zug was the associate-minister of the Jackson-Bartlett Church. It is less than 16 miles from my house.

Call it fate, luck, serendipity or an act from above. What are the odds that a couple who had been reading my weekly columns in a newspaper 4,700 miles away, would be rounding a corner in Denali National Park between 3 and 3:30 p.m. August 15th as a grizzly was deciding whether to have me as sushi or sashimi? This is amazing, imponderable.

Jeff and Wendy, I thank you again.

But too bad you didn't take pictures.

A bear encounter form is used by park officials to keep track of human/bear getting acquainted sessions. It is a four-page document and I was filling it out at the visitor center at the park's entrance.

Some of the questions are fairly straight forward. Name and address is fairly easy, as are questions about the time and location of the encounter. You are asked to identify yourself in terms of visitor, park employee, climber and professional photographer. You are given a list of activities you were engaged in prior to the encounter.

The list includes overnight hiking, day hiking in the backcountry, walking on road, hiking on maintained trail, driving on the road, camping and other. There wasn't a choice for bicycling. I circled "other" and wrote in "cycling road."

Then the park people get a little picky. First, they ask the type of bear. The choice were grizzly, black or unknown. I circled grizzly.

Then came color identification. Possible hair colors were blond, light brown, medium brown, dark brown, black and unknown. I circled both blond and light brown.

The next three questions had to deal with size, age and sex of the bear. Given a choice between small, medium and large, I pondered the size of my bear friend. It seemed huge, especially since I was 50 to 75 feet from the jaws and claws of death. Small, no grizzly is small when it is just you and the grizzly. I circled medium.

Age was one I couldn't ascertain. There certainly wasn't time to ask the bear for its drivers license or passport. It didn't look like a cub, nor a yearling which were two choices. Then came sub-adult, which is probably scientist talk for teen-ager, and adult. Again, since I really hadn't been up close and personal with either, I couldn't be sure. I circled unknown.

Then there was the question of sex. I didn't look. I didn't care. I circled unknown.

The multiple choice questions continued. What was the bear doing when first observed? Traveling, I circled. What were you doing prior to seeing the bear? Bicycling, I wrote. What was the bear's initial reaction? Walked towards people, I circled. What did you do then? I circled both backed away and made noise. Prayer was not an option to be circled.

Curious about the aftermath of the grizzly meeting, I contacted Denali National Park officials to find out what happened to the bear. They wrote back: "Based on the description of the bear-human interaction, we determined the bear acted in a curious manner, therefore, no aversive management action was taken."

In other words, they didn't kill the bear.

There were 194 reports of bear/human interactions in Denali National Park during 1994. I was one of them. Also during that summer, of those 194, four of them were meetings between bear and bicyclists on the Park Road. There were no bear/biker conventions in 1993.

Of those four meetings, two were reported as encounters. That means that the bear knew of a human presence, but didn't do much about it. There isn't any contact. The bear is neutral. The other two meetings were reported as incidents. That's what mine was. That means there's contact or some sort of aversive action had to be taken. Being saved by a couple of folks in a pick-up made the meeting quite an incident.

The End
of the Road

Global Odyssey

What would you do if a border guard wouldn't let you into the country? How would you react if a newspaper photographer asked you to pose naked for the paper? What would you do if you were a female in a rest room and a man sauntered in, naked?

All of these situations happened to a pair of women cyclists from Belgium during the first bicycle trip they every took. On April 8, 1990, Ingrid DeWilde and Nicole Dierckx left their home in Antwerp, Belgium. They were heading for China. They didn't get back until August 30, 1991. Along the way they traveled nearly 10,000 miles and visited countries like the former Yugoslavia, Turkey and Russia. They even wrote a book about it. It's in their native language which is Dutch. It's called "14,809 Kilometers with a Bicycle to China." That's the rough translation anyway. They said they sold 5,000 copies of it.

That trip wasn't enough for the adventurers. They had to do it again. But how do you top that? Pretty easy. Pedal around the world.

And that's what these two 29-year-old's were doing in Alaska when I met them in a restaurant in Cantwell. The town is roughly midway between Fairbanks and Anchorage on the George Parks Highway. The Parks Highway is a picturesque road that winds along towns like Nenana where people actually bet big money on when the ice breaks up and starts to flow every spring. It also runs to Talkeetna where each spring many intrepid alpinists catch small planes to base camp for their ascent of Denali. DeWilde and Nierckx left Antwerp April 9 on a four-year, 50,000 mile sponsored global odyssey.

"One of the most important rules is we have to stay together. Even when we have a fight, we have to stay together. Even when someone goes to the toilet, someone has to stand outside and watch. You feel more safe," said DeWilde.

The two are great friends and have been together so much over the past few years, that they finish each other's sentences. They are happiest when they are on the road. Nicole seems happiest when there is food, plenty of food, and shopping. Ingrid is the one who handles the finances.

Being two women on a worldwide adventure has meant taking a few precautions. They have bicycle alarms, carry pepper spray and have learned kick boxing and karate. They have had to use the spray and martial arts on the road.

During their ride to China, they went through Islamic countries. There they had to don, and pedal in, long dresses and headgear so as not to break with custom. In Turkey, a newspaper photographer asked them to pose nude in front of their bicycles for a picture. They compromised on swimsuits.

Chinese border guards wouldn't let them into the country. What are two girls to do? Cry, of course. It worked.

Could a guy do that?

"We don't know, we're not guys," the two answered in unison.

In the former Yugoslavia, they stayed at the home of a single man. Ingrid had just finished taking a shower and Nicole was preparing to take hers, when the host entered the bathroom in the buff and attempted to rape Ingrid, according to the pair.

Nicole ended up smashing a window and throwing a chair outside to get help. That unfortunate situation forced them to have another rule: "As a rule, we now stay with families," said Nicole.

But they still share the road with men and made an exception to their rules by sharing a campsite with me for two nights.

The two average about 50 miles a day, have a budget of about $25 per day for the pair and have had much of their trip subsidized by sponsors. Once a month, they telephone a radio station in Belgium to do an interview and update the small country on their progress.

"We have traveled with guys. They like more to cycle. They are more interested in speeds and the distance. We like to enjoy every kilometer," said Ingrid.

"Guys don't like cities. They don't like to shop, you know," added Nicole with a contagious laugh.

For the pair, cycling is the ultimate way of travel. From Europe, they flew to Iceland and cycled the northern part of that country. Then it was a flight to New York that got them to the United States. They did not cycle across, but took a plan instead to Prudhoe Bay, Alaska, the northernmost town in the country accessible by road. They were bicycling from there to the tip of South America before on to other parts of the world.

"We have chosen to cycle because it is the best way to learn about the country and see how they live. When you are a tourist you don't see as much. You don't experience the country," said Nicole.

And what an experience these two will have in a country called America.

The Beginning of the End

Alaska's largest city, Anchorage, was a place to rest for a few days and take in both its urban sophistication and natural beauty. Located on the Cook Inlet, on clear days snow-capped mountains are seen in the distance. Miles of bicycle paths roll through the city. In the winter, they double as cross-country ski trails. They also provide easy access to get around the area. Moose apparently know no boundaries in Alaska. Touring around one neighborhood, I came upon two moose eating the leaves from the trees of an immaculate home smack in the city confines. Museums and restaurants called. After pedaling so many miles, the legs and muscles relished another form of exercise — walking.

At this time, a decision had to be made where to end the trip. Two possibilities evolved — Homer and Seward. Both were located on the Kenai Peninsula. There would reach a point in both communities where the road would end and be replaced by the sea. Alaskans are mad about fishing. There appears to be no freezer in any home that does not have locally caught halibut or salmon. Down by the docks, I could get a closer look at this part of Alaskan life.

There was really one factor that made me choose Seward over Homer — distance. Homer was 233 miles away, while Seward waited for me 127 miles away.

The road to get there was the Seward Highway. The scenic, narrow route follows the Turnagain Arm portion of Cook Inlet before heading inland and ending at Resurrection Bay. Glistening mountains and glaciers stood by the road for the rider to pass by. Wide valley's made the eye search for miles. The clouds battled with the mountain tops for supremacy in the sky. The trails of the Alyeska Ski Resort could be seen in the distance. The Bird House, a tiny bar with shavings on the floor and business cards and patron's underwear stapled to the walls was the place for a beer. I didn't have any underwear, so I left a business card in a bra.

Along the way there are many areas to stop and learn more about the area, or just gaze at the sea. At one point, it is encouraged to scan the horizon for beluga whales. The beasts must have been under water that day.

Glaciers stand mighty. They call out. One such mammoth, the Portage Glacier, was the night's first stop a few miles off the highway. Hiking in the cool snow while the sun beat down about the traveler's brow is a confusing experience. But all one has to do is reach down to the ground, pick up the snow and use it as a natural air conditioner. Some snow looked blue. Other snow, underneath layer upon layer of snow, must have been hundreds, no thousands, of years old. There snow melted to water and fed the sea. The sea is home to life which feeds man. There was nature's cycle for all to see, just in a little snowball that fit into a hand.

From sea level, the road reached upward to Turnagain Pass and an elevation of 1,000 feet. Clearly this area is a place where Alaskans play. Trailheads invited hikers in. The mountains looked enticing for winter skiing. Fishermen cast their lines in countless streams.

Fish — there is always fish. The salmon were running this time of year. Starting thousands of miles away, they fight against the current to return home to their spawning grounds. They are grand beasts these pink, red and silver salmon. From many a bridge, they could be seen during the final leg of their most amazing journey. Cramped together for space, 10, 20, 30 of them competed for oxygen and energy in the throes of death. How nasty some were, snapping at each other with ugly, large teeth.

Others had already laid their eggs and died. Their foul-smelling carcasses would line the banks. The bodies had been picked clean by birds and bears. Eyes were picked and sometimes all that remained were skeletons or half-eaten fish.

For many a creature in Alaska, journey's end is at water's edge, I thought as I fell asleep that second night.

One more day remained.

The End of the Road

T he journey ended as it began — by the sea. This was not the familiar Atlantic. Now, after 5,198 miles and 10 flats, the wheels were now on the rocky shores of the Pacific in Seward's Resurrection Bay.

The day was cloudy with temperatures in the mid-50's just like May 2 in Portland, Maine, the day this cycling odyssey began. I wheeled my bicycle into the frigid waters. A few photos were taken.

That was all.

Amazingly, the front tire was the same one that started the journey from one side of the continent to the other, from America to Canada and back again. The tire had been through rain, snow, hail, dirt, mud, dust and sun. It had held the weight of a weary rider and his equipment over ever-changing terrain for 116 days through , five states, six provinces, and five time zones.

On Thursday, August 25 at 1:08 p.m., the rider ran out of road in a small port town on Alaska's Kenai Peninsula. There was happiness from the athletic achievement of the adventure and sadness at seeing the end of an amazing journey that provided a multitude of beauty from the land and its people. It was time for the trip to end.

Staring death in the face in Denali National Park had deflated the rider a bit. Familiarity called.

But there was a twist on that final day, another example of it-sure-is-a-small-world syndrome. To commemorate the end of the ride, I pedaled over to *The Seward Phoenix Log* office on Fourth Avenue to see if the editor might want to send a reporter down to the shores of Resurrection Bay, take a picture and do a story. The reporter, Eric Fry, was agreeable, but we would have to wait for the editor to get back from lunch. During our wait, Fry and I chatted. As it turned out we were both displaced New Yorkers. He was in Alaska, I was in New Hampshire.

"New Hampshire," he said. "My editor used to work in New Hampshire."

"What's his name?" I asked.

"Ed Carroll."

The name sounded familiar. Quite familiar, but I just couldn't place it. Journalists move around in their climb up and down the ladder of success. Names come and go.

Carroll returned from lunch and we were introduced.

"Have we met? Your name sounds familiar," Carroll said.

Carroll and I started to list the places we had worked. Then we both smiled. We found the connection. We agreed that we knew each other because we had read each other's bylines in New Hampshire newspapers. His was in *The Carroll County Independent*, a weekly newspaper that covered the town in which I lived. Mine was in *The Manchester Union Leader*, the statewide paper with a reputation for leaning to the right.

We also agreed that we might have met each other at an event or two. That was 5,000 miles and a few years ago.

Serendipity had struck again.

To celebrate the dipping of the wheels in the Pacific, I walked with my bicycle and gear up to a Chinese restaurant. There, I ordered and reflected on this four month ride.

The traveler is vulnerable on the road. Theft happens. It happened to me. I was fortunate. The Royal Canadian Mounted Police were able to find and return by bicycle helmet and riding glove within hours of it being stolen outside a Saskatchewan restaurant.

Weather can interfere with the best plans. When you are outside often, you realize how imperfect the days are. I found myself riding in conditions four months ago that called for beer, pizza and videos. Fear can follow you,too. Cyclists die. They are hit by cars. People and animals can rip open a tent and do serious damage to the occupant inside. But to succumb to fear is a mistake. That must not happen for then there is no journey, no discovery.

The closer I came to a metropolitan area, the more I was asked if I was afraid to be riding alone and if I was carrying a weapon. The only item I carried that could be considered a weapon was a Swiss Army knife. That is more a tool for spreading peanut butter and opening cans of tuna fish than inflicting harm. I do not know how to shoot a gun and have no desire to carry one while riding. Plus, Americans can't bring handguns into Canada. In hindsight, a can of pepper spray is a good idea.

Some things I might have done differently. I could have improved on the water-carrying system I had — three water bottles. Water bottle holders can carry commercial quart-sized soft drink bottles. That would carry more liquids. There are also straw and on-the-back systems I could have experimented with. A device that could keep water cool would be appreciated too.

Carrying a spare tire is a necessity for the Alaska Highway and far northern roads. I didn't carry one and found out the hard way you need it. But a credit card and phone book can also get you out of a jam in some remote places. White t-shirts on a bike trip is a no-no. Duct tape is essential. The front saddle bags could have been bigger since my computer took up a full rear pannier. Both a flashlight and candle lantern were unnecessary. The flashlight was used back in May and again recently as summer daylight is long in the Land of the Midnight Sun. Carrying a tarp would have been a good idea too. It doubles as ground cloth and quick rain shelter. A canister of white gas more than 11 ounces would have been better too.

Traveling with a computer is fun. Bicycling the information highway and getting e-mail from two countries, friends and strangers is fascinating. Rodeman thanks you all. Next time I would use an acoustic coupler that fits over a telephone receiver instead of one that plugs into a wall. That way you would use pay phones instead of hotel phones.

Physically, I am stronger now after nearly 60-mile days. My body is 20 pounds lighter. Let's see if I can retain some of this newfound wealth. The miles have taught me that television can be an evil ruler. Books are good. Talking to people is good. Making meals should be a time to share. Time can be made for things you enjoy if you aren't swayed by the remote control.

Don't fight the miles. Goals are sometimes set arbitrarily. They can be broken just as easily. If the body says no, listen. Subsequently, if the body says yes, ride on.

Underneath though, a journey of this length and magnitude touches deeper issues. There is no escape from yourself when you're on the road. Nothing can prepare you for what you might discover, for what you might like and dislike about yourself. Mental, as well as physical aptitude, is tested. Your confidence builds. Your character grows.

The adventure also touches other people. It awakens their feelings of journey's past. Youth is revisited. Dreams are remembered. Those who have traveled pay back in the form of kindness for generosities bestowed upon them earlier in life. Those with wanderlust in their hearts who live without the means of travel choose you to wander the roads for them during a vicarious vacation. People who are curious invite you into their homes, to their dinner tables.

The most rewarding part of this journey was the people — both the loved ones and friends who supported me at home and the new ones who took me into their homes and lives. The new friends gave me glimpses into worlds alien to me. They shared. They gave. The serendipitous encounters I experienced still are mind-boggling. I can only hope I gave those who followed and were part of this ride something in return. Perhaps it is the spark for your own adventure.

Travel is renewal. By 30, we are supposed to be set in our lives with a good job, wife or husband, mortgage, kids and a kitchen filled with conveniences that are designed to make our lives easier but really make us work more so we can attain them. That is suffocating for some. I learned from this journey that I am living the only type of life that makes sense to me. I must embrace who I am rather than be stuffed into a pre-cast mold.

Still, I only saw and experienced a very small part of a very great land. Each road I didn't cycle is another tale, another world to see. The trip could have been much different. What would have happened had I taken the low roads from North and Thunder Bays? How had the day might have been different if I spent just five more minutes with a cup of coffee at a lodge? What if I had camped in that spot over there, instead of this one over here?

And I only stuck to the roads. There are paths to hike, rivers to paddle.

Roads lead to a small portion of what there is to see.

So with these thoughts, the fortune cookie came.

Inside was this: "Your happiness is entwined to your outlook in life."

This was true I thought as I walked around Seward's waterfront with its fishing tour operators, restaurants and boats. I leaned my bike against a bench to sit and look at the water. I looked over at my bike.

We had reached the end of the road...for now.

The author reaches the end of the road in Seward, Alaska on August 25, 1994. He rode into Resurrection Bay, ending a 5,198 mile cycling adventure. (Photo by Eric Fry/The Seward Pilot Log).

About the Author

Marty Basch has written about the outdoors and travel for many newspapers and magazines throughout the United States and Canada. His articles have appeared in *SKI, Fodor's Travel Guides, Cross-Country Skier, Yankee, The Montreal Gazette* and other publications.

He has worked as an overseas radio reporter, covering the Palestinian uprising for CBS News. A bicycle touring veteran, he also has won four Associated Press awards for his work in broadcast journalism and the Harold Hirsch Award for Excellence in Ski Writing presented by the North American Ski Journalists Association. Basch is a member of the Explorer's Club. He lives in New Hampshire when he's not on the road with his computer.